Colleen

I am so blesse
in my life
May you continue on your path
Have faith hope & love
always
Earl Grinnett

# Survival
## on a Wing and a Prayer

**Gail Lionetti and
Janet Cunningham, Ph.D.**

authorHOUSE™

*1663 LIBERTY DRIVE, SUITE 200
BLOOMINGTON, INDIANA 47403
(800) 839-8640
WWW.AUTHORHOUSE.COM*

First published by AuthorHouse 11/12/05

ISBN: 1-4208-9252-5 (sc)

Printed in the United States of America
Bloomington, Indiana

This book is printed on acid-free paper.

Cover art: Gerard M. Guillot

# Acknowledgments

**From Gail:**

For all those in the spirit world, who have come to give closure to the loved ones here on Earth.

For my grandson Gavin, whom I have not yet met at this writing – I want you to know how I have a light in my heart lit for you and have purchased a star in the universe in your name. You are loved so very much and know one day we will be together.

Janet Cunningham - Without meeting you this book wouldn't have been possible. I want to thank you for your time and patience, support and loyalty and learning to understand me. I love you Janet, from deep within my heart.

John Dougherty - Thank you for always being there for me in so many ways; your heart is so big. You are always smiling, caring and giving. I am so blessed to have you as my friend.

Jeff Ryan - Thank you for taking me into my past lives, for you brought me much understanding of why my life this time around with my mother was so upsetting. Now I have closure and my life can go on, forgiving her for what I went through.

Chris Kirschman, my Metropolitan Life Insurance man, since retired - You knew of my childhood and my early adult life with marriage, life struggles. You always said, "When are you going to write that book?" Well Chris, here it is. You, too, have many struggles and I pray that you will continue to be strong. I thank God for putting you into my life and giving me the courage to go on. Now I ask God to give you the strength and courage to go on in your life, and I know He will. God Bless, Chris.

Barbara and Joe Strauss, my neighbors - Joe has since passsed on but his memory will remain close to my heart. He always worried about me, but through the strength he sends me I get through many things, (and Joe stop playing with my paper towels). Barbara, I thank you so much for being there for me and taking care of my cats; we all appreciate it very much. You are both loved.

My teacher from Raritan High School Mrs. Decker-Byrne - I want to thank you for always trying to help and give me the encouragement to go on. You are the best and will always have a special place in my heart. God bless you.

John Jennings - You will always have a special place in my heart. I can't thank you enough for being my spiritual guidance teacher. Thank you for giving all your time and attention to me when I needed it; may God continue to always bless you.

Scott Cunningham - Thank you for allowing me to share your home and Janet with me in the times I have come to do this book. I always felt a sense of peace with you and loved your hugs. I will always keep you and Janet close to my heart. God Bless.

Thank all those who have so much faith in me, believe in me and show love and caring. The cards, letters and emails allow me to go on and help others. I am ever so grateful that God sent me back to bring joy and peace in the hearts of all who come to me.

To all my staff of *Angels Among Us* - Without all your support, time and effort, my dinners would not be a success. I never had to worry about the jobs all of you were assigned to do. You did them without a hitch, and for that I am ever so grateful.

Most and foremost, my guides - If it weren't for them I would have lost my sanity a long time ago. Grey Wolf keeps me smiling with his humor; Chief White Feather stands next to me and shows me my spiritual path; White Eagle and Eagle are always with me when I travel protecting me from any harm, along with my two hawks and black crows who I call Heckle and Jeckle. Lakota my buffalo whom I want to apologize for the first name I gave him, not knowing why he wouldn't communicate with me until I changed his name. While writing this book, I found the answer. I am ever so sorry. Know that I truly love and appreciate all of you for being here for me and giving me the guidance I need.

**From Janet:**

To Scott, my husband of 33 years, or 2 years, depending on how we count. Thanks for your support through the writing of this book...keeping the refrigerator filled, and understanding during the Sunday through Tuesday intensive writing sessions when Gail and I were "glued" to the computer. I appreciate and love you.

To Gail – Our acquaintance was very new when we began the partnership for this project. During this time we have struggled with words, sentence structure, concepts and beliefs...we have laughed together and cried together...yet there has never been a conflict in respect, trust, and honoring each other and our work in the world. You are truly a very special lady—honest, caring and generous, with a big heart and desire to help people in need. I truly wish that you are able to find "heaven on earth." You deserve the very best that life can offer.

**From both of us:**

To our special readers, Karen Wildt, Ginger Bower, and Sarah Bower – Thanks so much for your help and feedback.

Jerry Guillot - We deeply appreciate your professional expertise, creativity, and kindness with re-doing all of the photos and documents in this book...and for the beautiful front cover. Thank you so much!

This book is dedicated to Chris Kirschman
who always said to me,
"When are you going to write that book?"
- Gail Lionetti

# TABLE OF CONTENTS

# Introduction

      Gail Lionetti and Janet Cunningham met in 2004, brought together by a friend for a potential business project. Since Janet would be driving from Maryland to New Jersey, Gail invited her to stay in her home overnight after the meeting ended.

      Although the initial business project was short-lived, a growing friendship developed between Gail and Janet. In fact, at their first meeting they stayed up talking until after 2:00 am. During the sharing about their personal and professional lives, they realized that Gail's dream of writing her story could be complemented by Janet's expertise; she had already authored several books. Janet is president of *Heritage Authors®,* a business that encourages people to document their stories to be handed down to their children and grandchildren.

      In addition to her expertise as a writer, Janet is also a therapist, specializing in regression therapy—taking people back into childhood memories and also past lives. This would give Gail the "safe space" that she needed to relive the painful experiences of her life. Gail knew that writing her story would bring up hurt and pain; it would not be an easy process for her to go through. Gail's spirit guides immediately joined the conversation, encouraging the collaboration.

      Janet has also worked with many psychics, some in her own research to understand how the mind works in psychic/intuitive information. She has also assisted some psychics and mediums to expand their abilities – and has helped others to become more grounded and balanced with their gifts.

We have written this book with "two voices."

      Janet's writing appears in type such as this, usually at the beginning and/or end of each chapter. Janet shares thoughts related to Gail's story, as well as teaching elements related to psychic perception, past lives, and research in consciousness.

Gail, telling her story, appears in type such as this, and of course, is the heart of the book.

Any book about a person's life needs to have a purpose that goes beyond flattering one's ego. Gail's desire is to share her story in order to help others. She stresses that a person can always turn their life around...to heal from the *darkness* of the past and to create more *light* in the present.

> "The purpose of my writing this book is to let others know that no matter what you go through in life—including great pain and hardships—one can succeed in whatever they set out to do. As I take you through my life's journey, I hope you will find the healing that I have found through many years."

It is our desire to share our experiences and, through Gail's story, to give encouragement that—by connecting to your spiritual path—you can fulfill your own destiny.

Many blessings on your path-
Gail Lionetti and Janet Cunningham
December 2005

# Survival

Today, Gail Lionetti does shows for a couple of hundred attendees; she prefers that the number not exceed what she can reach for personal attention. Before each event, she prays to God and asks that her guides be with her in order to help the people who have come, anxious to hear a message from their loved ones who have passed over. During the show, she calmly walks around the room, listening to spirits of the deceased, as well as hearing from her spirit guides who help her in giving the messages appropriately—occasionally urging her to stop the message until there is a more private setting for the receiver.

Who would ever guess that not long ago, Gail vehemently fought her gift, believing that *psychic* meant *witchcraft*?

How did she go from a deep-seated fear about witchcraft to accepting her psychic gift as coming from God?

Gail's story is one of survival:

- survival from physical, emotional and mental abuse from her mother
- survival from an unhappy marriage
- surviving the task of raising two children as a single mother
- survival as a corrections officer and private investigator
- surviving two cancer operations
...and, surviving two near-death experiences.

During childhood and through adult years, Gail hated her mother with a vengeance.

How did she go from deep anger towards her mother to acceptance and forgiveness?

During high school years, Gail was a bully, physically and mentally abusive to her classmates.

How did she go from a young person filled with rage to an adult overflowing with love for others and a desire to serve?

This is a story of transformation from:

- fear to love
- hate and hurt to forgiveness
- rage against others to service in helping others in pain

Gail had two near-death experiences that changed her life; however, it seems that her life experiences, the day-to-day struggles and life lessons, have been the moving force in her transformations. That may be true for all of us. It is our life experiences—how we respond to them—which cause us to grow, or to stay stuck.

As we move further into the 21st century, more and more people are having transpersonal and spiritual experiences. The word "transpersonal" refers to those things which go beyond the personal or physical realm—experiences such as sensing the presence of a deceased relative, having a pre-cognitive dream (a dream of something that actually occurs in the future), psychic knowing, visions, and other paranormal events. Sometimes the transpersonal experience also involves a spiritual awakening.

Until very recently all psychological evaluations and diagnoses of such experiences fell into the categories of hallucination, delusion, psychotic, or schizophrenic and the person was commonly given drugs...sometimes even confined to an institution. Orthodox psychology and psychiatry had no understanding of spiritual experiences; in the medical field, they simply did not exist.

Ever so gradually, people in the medical field are accepting that transpersonal or spiritual experiences exist...and exist among people who are well-balanced, fully functioning in society, and do not need traditional psychotherapy. In fact, these spiritual or transpersonal awakenings are leading us into the next level of consciousness— they are expanding us beyond the limitations represented by our five senses.

At the same time, it is important to recognize that some people do lose connection to reality. We have examples of people who have murdered, saying that God told them to do it. It is necessary, therefore, to be able to discern the difference between a person who is delusional or psychotic, and one who is following his/her spiritual path. Of course, any spiritually awakened teacher will admit to being "imperfect." If a teacher claims to have all the answers, I'd encourage a critical consideration of the teachers' ego and actions.

How does one tell the difference? Perhaps one of the best answers, paraphrased from the Christian Holy Bible is "...by their fruit you will know them."[1]

Based upon my work and experiences, I think it is essential that a person be mentally and emotionally grounded and functioning well in society *before* exploration into out-of-body experiences or psychic phenomena. Nevertheless, sometimes these transpersonal or spiritual experiences *come to us* – and they are life altering.

After her surgery, Gail was told that she had approximately 6 months to live. She had been working two jobs in order to support herself and her children; now she was unable to work at all. Again and again, she prayed to God to let her live for her children, pleading that she would do whatever he called her to do, if he would show the way.

After her prayers, she met Helen, a psychic who used her gifts to work with police on murder cases. Helen told Gail that she could use her abilities in a similar way.

What would *you* do if the way shown to you by God was diametrically opposed to your religious beliefs? Gail had talked to spirits since she was a child; these voices were her friends and she had no reason to question them. However, in her mind, she made a distinction—using psychic abilities were connected to witchcraft.

At this, Gail faced a major dilemma. Was God leading her to use her psychic gifts to help people in this way? But...this, Gail had always believed, was witchcraft. In fact, fear of witches had bothered her all of her life; she had even called her mother a witch.

What was she to do?

---

[1] Matthew 7: 17-20, Holy Bible: From the Ancient Eastern Text, 1933.

# Why Does Mommy Hate Me?

Is it possible for us to know, in the womb, the circumstances of the mother and father we are being born to? Current research in consciousness says, yes, and I have regressed (taken people back in memory) many people who have memories of being in the womb.

While in the womb, we have two streams of consciousness: that of the developing fetus and also a higher wisdom or "Higher Self." We might also call it the "soul."

The fetus is developing according to the genes of parents and ancestors; the physical shell, brain, and DNA that will house the soul is being created.

Our higher mind/spirit exists outside of our physical body and physical brain. This higher wisdom is that of the spirit which carries greater knowledge—that of the soul's purpose and intentions for this lifetime. In fact, sometimes our spirit is still linked to the intention or plan for this incarnation. For some people, there is still awareness of the soul's plan while in the womb. For others, however, the memories have already begun to fade.

Research has shown that the higher consciousness of the developing fetus has awareness, including a sense of joy and happiness in incarnating and being with its future family...or dread and fear.

Gail seems to have had a sense, while in her mother's womb, that she didn't want to be here...that being born to this mother would mean a torturous life for her. As you will learn, it was exactly that.

As Gail shares her story today, she can see that there was a greater purpose underlying her painful childhood memories...but that understanding wouldn't come until many years later, well into adulthood and after acceptance of her psychic gifts.

Let's not get ahead of ourselves; let's begin with reading Gail's words and learning what she lived as a child.

I was born to Mary and Gifford Hallam on November 5, 1950 at the Margaret Hague Hospital in Jersey City, New Jersey.

As I was in my mother's womb, I felt that I didn't want to be there – that I didn't want to be born to this woman. My soul must have sensed, while in the womb, that I was coming out to a torturous life, but chose to come anyway, because there were many lessons that I had to learn.

**Mother and Father**

As a child, no matter what I did, it was never right in my mother's eyes; therefore I was constantly getting beatings. It didn't matter what caused her anger; she found fault and found a way to harm or beat me. For example, in our cellar, we had a "coal bin." My mother would take me downstairs while she shoveled coal into the furnace. Often, she would beat me there – by pulling my hair and smacking me in the face. I never understood what I had done that was wrong.

As a child, I loved eating Quaker Puffed Rice for breakfast. Not knowing the difference between sugar and salt, I decided to take salt and mix it in with the sugar. My mother loved coffee, and the next morning when she put sugar in her coffee, it didn't taste right. She couldn't wait for me to put the sugar on my cereal. Loving sugar, I put lots of it on, and at my first taste of the cereal I thought I'd die. She knew what I had innocently done. Still, she told me that I couldn't leave the table until I ate every bit of that cereal.

Certainly even that pales when I compare it to my punishments when I said a bad word. Not knowing what I was saying, she made me eat—eat—a whole cake of Ivory soap. It happened more than once...because I never knew what I was saying that was wrong. I must have heard some "bad word" from someone.

She used to buy crabs and cook them in a pot. One fell on the floor and was running all around. It ran somewhere where we couldn't find it. She told me that when I went to sleep it was going to find me. I was petrified that it would get in my bed and claw me. My mother just didn't know the fright and the horror that she instilled in me. When she put the crabs into the hot boiling water, I wondered if she would ever do that to me. In my eyes, it was torture, torture to the crab. I was becoming so used to being tortured.

**Gail as Flower Girl**

One of my happy memories was going to Garfield Park with my little red wagon, sitting in it, and steering down a winding path. That was so much fun for me. I'd keep walking up the hill to go back down. Getting lost in playing, when I did go home, I got beaten once again because I didn't come home on time. But what was time? I didn't even know how to tell time.

As I look back on it now, there was no adult or older sibling who was able to comfort me after the beatings. My sister was 15 years older, and already living outside of the house. My mother sometimes beat me with a belt. I had welts that people noticed, but to my knowledge, no one ever questioned it.

A favorite memory of little girls is dressing up in their mother's clothes and high heels. Well, I hated wearing dresses, however I was a flower girl at the age of 6 at my sister's marriage. I had to wear a dress. It was full length, powder blue and I wore a tiara on my head. I felt like a queen and so important when I wore that dress and tiara.

When I was in Brownies we had a Halloween party and I walked 10 blocks in that dress and high heels to get to the party. People looked at me, saying how beautiful I was. I had never been told how beautiful I was; at least not by my mother.

When the party was over, I walked those 10 blocks back, again hearing friendly comments about how beautiful I looked. I felt so proud and happy until I got home, when I was reminded of how ugly I was, that no one liked me, and that I could do nothing right. I ran crying into the sun porch where my dolls were. There I could be assured that I was beautiful and that I was somebody.

My father, whom I loved so very much, was a Navy career man. I did not know him well because he was always on ships and away at sea. When he did come home, he always hugged me. I hugged him back and didn't want to let go. It was so sad for me when he had to go back to the ship. I used to look out to the sky and say to God, "Please let me be there if anything happens to my daddy." The day that he died—30 years later—it turned out that I was the only one there.

One day while I was in kindergarten at PS-20 (public school No. 20) and in the school yard, my teacher, Miss Bouquet, found me standing alone crying. She asked me what was wrong. I told her that my daddy got killed by a cannon ball. (I have no idea why I said that; I must have seen something on TV about a ship with a cannon ball and seeing people dying). My teacher took me into the office, called my mother, extended their sympathies and told them I was very upset and asked if she could come to get me.

**Gail in Kindergarten**

When my mother arrived, instead of explaining to me that my father was alive and okay, she pulled my arm as we walked 12 blocks home. In those 12 blocks, I got beaten by her fists, my hair pulled and lifted off the ground as she swung me by my hair. I never knew what I did wrong.

I became very attached to a brown teddy bear that my father once gave me. I felt that when I held that teddy bear I was holding my father. I felt so close to it; I'd cry to the bear, asking, "Why does my mommy not like me?" No one could take that bear from me; wherever I went, he came too.

Eventually, the bear began to forewarn me when my mother was drinking, preparing me for the beating that was to come. I could lock myself either in my room or the sun porch so she couldn't get to me. If she saw me, anger came with it. So teddy and I became best friends. I felt love from him; when I hugged him I believed that I was hugging my daddy. It was almost like my daddy came through that bear when I needed him.

I had many conversations with my dolls and as I look back now, I realize it was the start of my communication with the spirit world. I talked to them and they told me that everything would be okay. How I wish that someone could have tape recorded those conversations. I often wonder what else was actually being said between me as a 6-year old child and the spirit world.

However, it was about that time that my mother repeatedly said that my sister dropped me on my head one time and that is why I was "nuts." For my own clarification later on in life, I asked my sister and she said that she never dropped me on my head. It could have been possible that my mother heard me speaking to my dolls and did think I was "nuts."

**Gail and Aunt Mae, First Holy Communion**

Being raised as a Catholic, I had to go to catechism in order to make my *First Holy Communion*. "Independent me" did not follow instructions. The day before making Communion at St. Paul's, we were to make our first confession to the priest. I decided to go home—I didn't want to stand in the long line with the other kids.

The next day, having been instilled with fear about sinning, I realized I had already committed my first sin. I was making my communion without a confession. I was so afraid that, now, in addition to my mother, God would be punishing me. Still, I took the chance and received the first host thinking that somehow God would come and yell at me. However, this time I would understand what I had done wrong.

In Jersey City, we lived in what was called a "railroad room." It described rooms that continually started from the kitchen and went straight down into successive rooms of a bedroom, second bedroom, living room. Below these rooms were stores; one was a barber shop. The kids used to go in to the barber shop to read comic books.

One day, when I was about 5 years old, the barber asked me to sit in the chair as I read my comic book. I vividly remember that he took my right hand, put the towel around it and proceeded to have me rub his genitals. Of course, I didn't know what I was doing, but before his ejaculation, he brought his penis up to my mouth. All I remember was this white cream coming and didn't know what it was. He cleaned me up and I left to go play with the kids.

I didn't understand what was happening, but it continued numerous times. When I started to get a little older, I knew something wasn't right because he told me not to tell anybody or I would be in trouble. I was certain that if I told, I would get beaten again. I never told anyone—especially not my mother because she would have said it was my fault.

Later in life, I learned that my mother was known to frequent the corner bar. As time progressed, she became an alcoholic. A policeman would often bring her home. Growing up I was taught to feel safe and trust the policemen in our neighborhood. This policeman often came to our house; my mother said he was our uncle. I felt safe when he was in our home. With her getting drunk and nasty, I didn't have the fear of a beating during the times that he was there.

We moved from the railroad room two blocks to a two-family home on Wade Street where I had my own bedroom. As I'd lie in my bed at night I'd hear voices speaking to me. I wasn't afraid or scared because I felt safe and did not feel alone.

We had what we called a sun porch, going through two doors to get to it. I loved going out to that porch because I had all my dolls out there and my blackboard. I used to play school with my dolls.

While I taught them, I'd hear some answers come through. I loved being out on that sun porch because it was my safe haven. It was safe because I was further away from my mother; if she didn't see me, I didn't trigger her anger. I locked the door to the sun room. Of course, she could have come in, but because I locked it, I felt safe.

I was a "tom boy," playing with the boys, including my brother, on the block. We played stick ball, kick ball, and *I declare war.* It was a happy time for me; I looked forward to playing with the boys and could hold my own with them. There was a lot of pushing and shoving, especially in *I declare war,* however, as the only girl, I learned to give it right back.

As I walked to school alone, some kids picked on me and called me names. I soon learned that I could turn around and *wallop* them. At around age 7 and 8, I was beginning to become the *bully tom boy.* Soon the kids realized that they shouldn't mess with me.

In PS-34 I had a second-grade teacher named Miss. Eagen. To me, she looked like the wicked witch and I thought to myself, *No wonder she isn't married; she is a witch.* (I now think it could have been a possible past life memory). To me, she was mean and crabby with no personality. I hated to go to school, but when I did go, I couldn't be found in class. I found time to go to the bathroom and roam around the halls. When doing so, I would see spirits roaming with me so I thought it was okay not to go back to class. Well, my mother got a call.

Miss Eagen told her I would not stay in class, that I would go to the bathroom and not return. So, I guess after that discussion it was resolved that I couldn't go to the bathroom any more. So what is a kid supposed to do? I asked to go and was told no, so I went in my pants. I thought *I'll fix them.* Yea, right. Again, my mother was called to bring me a new set of clothes, which she did. But when I got home, I had to pay the price.

As I look back now, my mother never gave me any positive attention. So maybe that was a way of getting attention. I never felt any love from my mother, and wished so many times that my father could be home with me.

In my house on Wade Street the bedroom floor was real slippery. I used to lie on my stomach and slide back and forth pretending I was on a sleigh ride. The room was not big, but that little space gave me fun for those moments, just sliding back and forth.

**Gail in Cast with Sister and Mother**

Somehow my arm got caught underneath my chest and I broke it. I look back now and wonder, *How the heck did that happen?* Still it did. So, I had to go to Greenville Hospital to get a cast put on. When I got home, I was dragged by the hair on my head from the living room to the kitchen, for breaking my arm.

I had two good friends (when I was not playing with the boys), Margaret Keating and Mary Ann Byrne. We played dolls together and I used to ask them if they heard their dolls talking to them. Of course, they said no. So I thought that my dolls were special because I was the only one who had talking dolls. Back then they didn't sell talking dolls like they have today.

Mary Ann had a brother, John, who looked funny to me and wasn't like the rest of the kids. John was always with Mary Ann and played with us. He was such a funny kid. John was retarded. I will never forget his smile. I liked being around him; I felt safe with him. I couldn't understand why John went to a different school. It was called A. Harry Moore and it was for special children; that's all I knew.

As we grew up, we made fun of those special kids. It was like a stigma—if a kid went to A. Harry Moore, s/he was retarded. I never knew what that meant, but kids were—and still can be—cruel.

I recall seeing my first visualization of a spirit when Margaret's dad passed away. I was only 7 years old; my mother took me to the funeral home. I wasn't scared because I didn't understand what death was. She made me to go up to the coffin with her, telling me that he was sleeping. I saw Mr. Keating lying in the coffin, but didn't understand why he was also standing next to it. I couldn't help but think how handsome he was, as I heard him say, *Don't worry about me, Gail, I'm okay.* Of course I didn't dare tell anybody.

When I look back at old photos, there are several of me with a man and a woman, who I think were my godparents. I recall that I was in a car with them on the front seat, feeling tired and was told to lie down on the woman's lap and put my legs on the man's lap. The man, while driving, proceeded to run his hands up my legs and touch me in a way that I didn't like. Once again, I didn't understand and never said anything to my mother because it would have been my fault.

As my mother continued to accuse me of things that I didn't do and beat me, my hate for her began to build. Often, I just wanted to turn around and wallop her, as I did the kids who had hurt me. A lot of times I wouldn't go straight home from school; I'd wander around because I hated to see her face. I just wanted to run away.

When I did threaten to run away, my mother told me that she would put me in a home with the nuns. They would make me get on my hands and knees and scrub the bathroom floors with a toothbrush. I didn't know which choice was worse, being with the "witch" or the nuns. They both wore black and had control over me.

I seldom saw my father when he came home because he came in around 1:00 am on a Saturday morning and left at 2:00 pm on Sunday. In that time span, he needed to spend time with me and my brother, and also with his wife.

When I got my first 3-wheeler bike, my daddy took me to Roosevelt Park to teach me how to ride. As little as it sounds, it was such a joy for me. He also took me ice skating at the same park in the winter time. I asked my mother for hot cocoa; she said no, but my father bought it for me, anyway.

◊◊◊

When a child has been abused, she or he quickly learns to open all senses available—hearing, seeing and sensing have to be on heightened alert. It becomes necessary to be on the look-out constantly to protect oneself. The mental, emotional, and physical abuse that Gail lived with daily, the uncertainty and confusion about why she was being punished, *built in* an observant and vigilant nature. She developed a personality that had to stay watchful to everything around her.

As a part of that openness (an "open energy field") as a child, Gail was able to perceive audio and visual communication from beyond the physical dimension. She had a childlike acceptance of these experiences, and did not question them. At the same time, she also had a mature awareness, which such children usually possess, that it is not safe to talk about these experiences. These communications gave her comfort and assurance that she would be okay, in spite of the hurt and even danger, that she was living. In many ways the comforting messages from her "unseen helpers" did help Gail to survive.

The beatings continued, and Gail's rebellion—although not open rebellion to her mother—began to show up in school. She also acknowledged to herself that she really hated her mother; yet, there was no where to go and no one to help.

One of her childhood friends recalls those times:

When my family and I moved into Hazlet (Woodland Park), I remember my parents commenting on this blonde lady who used to sit outside the model homes when they were being built and drink beer with the guys. She was there almost every day. I never realized until later on that the woman was Gail's mother. I guess I had not met her yet. I'm assuming it was during school hours but I was young and I'm not real clear on everything.

Even though her mother was very nice to me, I always used to wonder why she was so mean to Gail. Every time I would go over to her house Gail was either cleaning or doing dishes. I used to say to myself that I was glad that my parents did not ask me to do all of that.

I always thought that Gifford (her brother) took pleasure in putting her down. It was obvious that he was the "golden boy," but he was also very mean to her at times. I guess he figured it was okay since her mother treated her so badly. I do remember her hitting Gail and pulling her hair on occasion.

I remember riding in the back of her dad's pickup truck. I used to love to do that. I didn't know her father very well and he never really talked much, but I knew in my heart that he was a kind man

- Carol

◊◊◊

We finally moved out of the big city into the country, to a town called Hazlet, New Jersey. There was nothing but farms all around. My father had become a recruiter for the Navy and now lived at home.

There was one small school house and another being built. The first school that I attended was Middle Road School; I was in 4th grade. I went to school in dresses, wearing knee-high socks. My teacher, Mrs. Baynes, along with the school principal, called me out into the hallway, and asked me to roll down my socks. She had seen black and blue welts all over my legs.

When she asked me what happened, I told her my mother beat me with a belt. They looked at each other; then Mrs. Baynes commented, "Okay, you can roll your socks up and go back into class." Back in those days, children were hit...but this was so severe that they had called me out into the hall to ask what happened. Nothing was ever done.

When we moved into the newly-developing area, there were only two houses, one of which was mine. When another house was being built across the street, a friend and I went to the house with matches and newspapers to set a fire and roast marshmallows. We put the newspapers down as if we were building a bonfire and lit the match. We didn't expect the house to go up in flames. Terrified, we ran home like nothing happened.

A day or two later I got off the school bus and saw a state police car parked in front of my house. I thought *This must be my uncle who used to visit back in Jersey City.* When I got into the house, I asked my mother, "Is this my uncle?" She said, "No, he is here to talk to you." He questioned me about the fire in the house across the street. Of course I lied because I didn't want to get beaten; however, I did blame the girl who was with me. When the trooper went to the girl's house, she blamed me.

Our parents had to take us to the state police barracks to be questioned further. The guys looked 10 feet tall to me, and I was scared as hell. Of course, they knew we had done it; we were the only two kids in the neighborhood. Our parents had to pay for the damages. Once again, I got my beatings.

I had a favorite uncle, Pete, who was my mother's brother. He lived in New York and visited often. I loved it when he came down. Since I was constantly being punished and not allowed to go out, he kept me occupied. We played board games and cards; he even showed me some tricks with cards.

I didn't know until later in years that he had five children of his own. When he and his wife separated, the five children had been put into foster homes. I never understood what happened between my aunt and uncle in their separation, but, sadly, their children never experienced the love that he gave to me. Strangely, my cousins didn't know their father as well as I had. If it weren't for Uncle Pete coming to see us, I probably would have been locked up in my room. It was a sad day when my mother got the word that my uncle was found, dead, in his room. At age 12, I lost my game-playing buddy.

Our cat had a litter of kittens. My mother took the kittens and placed them in a paper bag. There was a pond around the corner from where we lived. My father drove her around the corner and as I watched from my front window, I saw my mother get out of the car, and throw the bag into the pond of water. It traumatized me. I felt so bad for the kittens; she had murdered them.

When I went to school my mother cut my hair so short—it was called a "bowl cut." Of course, kids teased me because I looked like a boy. Kids picked fights with me. Not only was I being tortured at home, I was being tortured outside the home, as well. When I told my mother that the kids picked on me and fought with me, she replied that I probably deserved it.

In contrast from the 4<sup>th</sup> grade, which I hated, I loved the 5<sup>th</sup> grade. I had a teacher, Mrs. Teague, who I liked because she gave me the attention that I needed. For the first time in my life, I felt like a "teacher's pet." She let me help with things in the classroom, such as clearing bulletin boards and washing blackboards. As little as it sounds, I felt important because I felt needed.

My friend, Margaret occasionally visited me from Jersey City and stayed for a few weeks during the summer. I remember my mother washing and waxing the kitchen floor. Margaret went to the refrigerator to get a bottle of milk. The glass bottle was heavy. It slid out of her hands, dropping on the floor and broke into pieces, milk all over the newly-cleaned floor. My mother became angry. She picked up another empty milk bottle and broke it over my head because Margaret had just ruined her clean floor.

Then she proceeded to pick up a broom and hit me with the broom handle. Action such as this was something that I was used to experiencing. When I washed dishes, including pots and pans, my mother inspected them. One time there was a pot that was not quite clean. She hit me on top of my head with it, which caused an indentation in the pot. Now, not only was the pot dirty...but I had also ruined it.

Sometimes my mother and I went back to Jersey City to visit relatives and friends. I always wanted to visit Margaret during those times. However, in order to get to her house, I had to walk by the barber shop where I had been molested. Even though I walked on the other side of the street, my head down, I saw the barber watching me out of the corner of his eyes. I felt so uncomfortable, and wondered if he was doing the same thing to another little girl.

In 6<sup>th</sup> to 8<sup>th</sup> grades, I went to Cove Road School. In 7<sup>th</sup> grade, I had a teacher, Mr. Sheehan. My desk was right in front of the room. Once again, I felt as if I were the teacher's pet, although this time it didn't last. Mr. Sheehan asked me to correct some of the school papers; he even sent me home with papers. It made me feel needed. I had good penmanship so he asked me to re-write some of his papers for college that he attended at the time. When my mother questioned it, I just said that he had asked me to re-write some papers for him.

One day, when Mr. Sheehan left the room, Barry, a boy in class who was always in trouble, spit on the teacher's suit jacket. When Mr. Sheehan came back to the room and saw this on his jacket, he yelled, "Who did this?" A few classmates replied, "Gail did it." Much to my surprise, Mr. Sheehan accused me even though I tried to tell him I hadn't done anything. After feeling so needed and valued by him, everything changed. He wanted nothing to do with me.

In 8th grade there was a slang term given to the way people dressed: kids were either "greasers" or "collegiates." Greasers wore black leather jackets; hair was well manicured compared to collegiates who looked like "nerds." Collegiates wore plaid shirts, kaki pants, and their hair was "out of sorts," like they just rolled out of bed.

In my school, greasers out-numbered collegiates. I wasn't a greaser and I certainly wasn't a collegiate, so I felt that I didn't fit in. I was constantly threatened, picked on, and in fights. Most of my 8th grade, I didn't want to go to school because I knew that one of the greasers was going to beat me up. I used to try to walk with my brother and his friends, but my brother wouldn't help me.

One day I was going to the movies with my friend, Linda, who I thought of as my "partner in crime." I suggested that we stop in the local grocery store and steal some candy for the movies, explaining, "Why pay for candy when you can get it free?" I proceeded to steal M&M's and other candy. I placed the packages under my arms underneath my coat.

As we walked out the door, the store manager was waiting for us. He slyly asked, "Is there anything that you forgot to pay for?" We both said no, and he directed us to his office. I was so scared that the candy fell out of my coat, and we were caught. When he asked for our home phone numbers, I made up a number. When he called and got the wrong house, he gave me a choice, "Either I call the police or I call your home." I wondered to myself, *what will be worse, the police arresting me or my family picking me up*—either way I was going to be in trouble.

The store manager called my home. My father came to get me; he slapped me on the shoulder, asking what I had done. I cried to him saying I was sorry. After we got home and my father went out of the house, my mother started to hit me. My nose had been broken during a baseball game with my brother and it still had packing in it. She hit me directly in my nose, breaking it once again. She then gave me a book about The Blessed Mother and told me to go to my room and read it. I didn't read it; however I talked to God and The Blessed Mother asking forgiveness.

My mother had a friend who lived in Pennsylvania who we frequently visited during the summers. Glen had a son, approximately 14 years old. When I slept on the couch at night, he slept on the floor next to me and took my hand and had me rub his genitals. I remembered the same feeling that I had with the barber, but still didn't understand what was happening. All I knew was that I didn't like it. Still, I never told anyone for fear of getting beaten.

One person did see one of the beatings. Back then, insurance agents came to the house to pick up monthly payments. Mr. Kirschman knocked on the door and heard my mother call out, "Come on in." When he walked in, he saw her beating me with a 3-inch black leather strap with metal studs on it. As she proceeded to hit me, the studs broke open my skin and I was bleeding. There was blood on my arm and blood on the back of my head. I could feel the blood on my back, sticking to my shirt.

He yelled out, "Mrs. Hallam, don't hit her like that!" Her reply was, "Mind your own business. She played hooky and she is going to pay for it." I don't think Mr. Kirschman will ever forget that experience; however, in those times, people didn't interfere in the private business of other families.

I had my first babysitting job around this time. I made $20 a week (2 hours a day for 5 days a week). For me, that was a lot of money. A friend who I went to school with lived across the street from where I babysat. One day I went to see her and we sat in her father's Volkswagen with the keys in the ignition. I was in the driver's seat and said to Laurie, "Let's turn the car on to listen to music."

The Volkswagen was a 3-speed. I decided to become brave at the age of 13 and drive the car down the street in first gear, which was the slowest I could go. Realizing I had to make a turn or I would pass my house, I made a sharp left turn and went up the curb heading towards a house. I realized I was going to crash into the house so I turned the wheel again and hit a telephone pole. When I really get nervous, I can't stop laughing. I laughed hysterically while my friend cried hysterically. We had just crashed her father's car.

We left the car there. She went home and I did, too. Of course, I didn't tell my parents what I had done. Soon Laurie's father was knocking on our door. He told my mother what happened. I had to apologize to Laurie's father and was punished immediately. My mother began taking my $20 babysitting money each week to pay for the car repairs.

In 1972, my brother got married and Laurie's parents were invited to the wedding. Her dad came up to me with a few drinks under his belt and reminded me of what I did to his car. I commented that I had to baby sit for nothing for years in order to pay him back. He advised me that he never charged my mother a penny; the insurance took care of it. I was so angry when he told me. My mother had lied to me and kept my money. I hated to go baby sitting because I wasn't earning any money. I was paying—I thought—for the car repairs.

My hatred for her became even stronger. Each day when I came home from babysitting, I went to my room and locked myself behind the closed door. I wanted nothing to do with her. She didn't care. Once again, I was in my own little world, feeling safe behind closed doors.

To prepare myself to make confirmation, I had to go to cate-chism. Once again, I became a sinner. Before going to church, my friend and I went to a local store and stole red pistachio nuts. We took them to the church, sat on chairs, eating nuts and throwing shells on the floor.

The next day, the Mother Superior got on the microphone and announced that someone had been eating red pistachio nuts. She stated that everyone had to go to the front of the church, row by row, stand in front of her and show their hands...because she knew someone had red fingertips and she would know who had made the mess. Obviously, I and my friend got caught with red fingertips. She scolded us, but we laughed back to our seats because she didn't know that we stole them.

It did affect me, however, because since God knew everything, he would have known that we had stolen things and taken them into a church. The Mother Superior said that when you commit sin, you will be judged by God and sent to hell. In this case, although my mother didn't find out about it, God knew and I felt that somehow I'd be punished by him.

In another instance, I did get caught. I told my mother that a friend and I were going to the Stations of the Cross at Holy Family Church on a Wednesday night. We were really meeting two boys. My mother, being the detective that she was, knew I wasn't going there, and knew that across from the church there were dirt mounds. We were hiding in the dirt mounds. In the dark, all I could hear was, "Gail, I know you're over there." My friends scattered because they knew what my mother was like, and they, too, were afraid of her.

Coming out of the dirt mound, I got in the thick, mucky, gray clay. By the time I got home, it had dried on me. I had to sit in a tub of hot water, clothes and all, to get it off. When I came out with my pajamas on, that's when the strap came out and I got beaten.

My father finally spoke up, "Don't beat her like that," and I was sent to my room. During that time, I may have had fewer beatings because he was now retired and lived in the house, but they were just as severe as before he was there.

Another time, my mother had been drinking and she took a hammer and walked around the neighborhood looking for me. She saw my friend, Linda, and asked where I was. Linda said she didn't know. My mother exclaimed, "When I find her, I'm going to take the claw of this hammer and put it through her head." Linda saw me and fearfully warned me about what my mother said. Of course, it scared the hell out of me, because I knew she would do it if she caught me. I ran home. My father was in the garage and I told him what Linda had said. He told me to stay in the garage with him until she came home.

When she got home, he went into the house with me and asked what she was doing with the hammer. She told my father she was going to fix something. He asked what she had said to Linda; she denied that she had said anything. My father took the hammer away from her. To this day, I don't know what provoked her other than the alcohol.

My own anger inside continued to build and build. One day I was on the lawn playing croquet with a friend when another girl, Donna Presti, came up the street and started to provoke me. I tried to ignore her, but she got the best of me. I threw the mallet down, went across the street, and proceeded to fight her. This was the one time in which my mother supported me. She came out and cheered me on. I felt good because I was no longer the punching bag. By the way, years after Donna had been my punching bag, she became my son's Godmother.

Although the spirit world seemed to have faded away for several years, now it began to come back. Walking to and from school, I carried on conversations—out loud, mind you—there was no one with me who could be seen. I would connect with the spirit world— my "imaginary friends"—and ask why the greasers and my mother hated me so much. I heard that I did nothing wrong, that I was a good person, and they would help me get through it. Many times they did.

◊◊◊

During early adolescence, Gail's opportunity for loving attention was severely limited; the one uncle who visited died when she was young. It's no wonder that when a teacher gave her minimal attention by allowing her to help clean blackboards, Gail loved her; the task made her feel as if she was contributing. She felt good when another teacher had her assist him, yet that relationship had a disturbing twist when the other kids blamed Gail for an event. It appeared that everywhere she turned for positive attention, she was turned away.

Notice that the one memory that Gail shares in which she received positive reinforcement and acceptance from her mother was when Gail beat up a girl while playing croquet. The acceptance from her mother apparently came from approval of the violence. For Gail, however, the experience of beating up the little girl meant that, for the first time, she felt a sense of power. We might say that it was negative power, using one's strength to hurt another. Nevertheless, it proved to be a way that Gail—at long last—began to have a sense of how she could stop being a victim.

# Abuse Escalates

By the time Gail reached high school, she had learned that the way to survive was to fight. Fighting—bullying others—was the only way that she had any sense of control over her life. And, she couldn't fight her mother, so anyone else was fair game.

In addition to her new sense of power, an overwhelming anger began to burst forth from Gail. This inner rage that she had been carrying needed an outlet, and it was released on classmates, or, in her words, "anyone who looked at me cross-eyed." Throughout her young life, she had known only violence at home, most often not understanding why she was being beaten or punished. Gail was living what she had been taught.

During this time, Gail did not have the spirit communication of previous years. Her attention had been drawn outward. She was out of the house more and her focus was on the external world.

◊◊◊

As if it hadn't been hard enough to be among classmates numbering 30, now I was facing high school with hundreds of kids. My fears rose because of the numbers; more kids meant more people to bully me.

I decided to "unzip my shell and step out." I wasn't going to allow anybody to make fun of me or abuse me, let alone put a hand on me. Raritan High School teachers and classmates would have to deal with me. They most certainly did.

If another student looked at me cross while I was walking down the hallway, they got it. I didn't have to have a reason to fight; if someone got in my way, that person was the unlucky one. After all, that's how I got my name, "Cassius Clay," in the yearbook.

I put the word out that I wanted to see a girl who was called "ugly Mary." There was no reasoning to any of it. The bully in me had come out full force. Mary got the word and tracked me down in the gym locker room. She asked me what I wanted to see her about. I told her to place the books that she was carrying on the sink and then explained that she was so ugly that I had to straighten her face out. I proceeded to punch her in the face, breaking her nose.

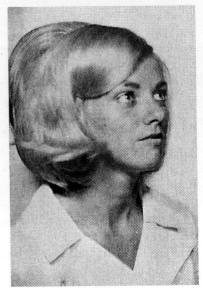

**Gail**

My gym teacher rushed in and immediately sent Mary to the nurse's office. She sat me down and asked why I had done it. I told her that it felt good. [Later on in life, I learned that Mary had been a foster child and a ward of the state. I looked back and felt so terrible for what I had done because this poor girl didn't have her own parents; they had given her up. She did not deserve that from me. I had my own tortures going on at home, and so did she. Yet, I had beaten an innocent person for no reason because she was a "weak one". I don't know where she is, but if she ever should read this book, I deeply apologize for what I did].

I was standing in the vestibule that connected to the gym locker room. There were 20 of us in this small space, waiting for the bell to ring to change class. A talkative Adeline, with a voice that irritated me, kept running her mouth. I told her to shut up. She kept it up and a fight ensued. I hated to have my hair pulled, and that's what she started to do.

We were both down in a bent position, with everyone surrounding us. I decided that I'd take my fist, come up in swing position and hit her in the face. Instead, when I came up, I hit my gym teacher.

Mrs. Decker (now Mrs. Byrne) exclaimed, "Gail, you just hit me!" Startled, I got up immediately; I felt so bad. Mrs. Decker was one teacher who I truly loved. She took me into the gym office, yelled at me, and said she had no other choice but to send me to the main office. Of course, I was suspended and my mother had to come to get me. When I got home, she punished me with the strap and I went to my room.

Every weekend, my mother found an excuse for me to be punished. On Fridays, my sister, Ginger, would often come to get me at school and take me to her house for the weekend so I could be away from my mother. Ginger truly was my angel.

Standing once in the girls' bathroom, we had the windows open. Between classes, a lot of girls went there to smoke. I didn't smoke, but apparently there was nothing better for me to do. I stood by the windows, took a book of matches and kept throwing the lit matches out the window.

All of a sudden, someone yelled, "The grass is on fire!" I turned around and looked out the window at the courtyard. It was engulfed in flames. Since the buildings surrounded it, the school had to be evacuated. The fire department came, extinguished the fire, and classes resumed as normal. They never figured out who did it. In this case, it hadn't been intentional; the grass had been very dry.

In Spanish class, I had a confrontation with one of my classmates and pushed her up against the blackboard. Without realizing it, I had my thumb into her throat, cutting off her breathing. When the teacher walked in and saw what was happening, he yelled at me, "What are you trying to do? Kill her?" I didn't realize it; she was turning blue.

The teacher wrote a letter for me to take to my mother saying that I was not behaving in class. Of course, I never gave her the letter. By not giving her the letter, I felt in control. The next day, the teacher asked if I'd given her the letter and I said yes. He asked what she said. I replied that she yelled at me and told me not to fight in school. Fortunately, he never followed up on it with her.

These were not isolated incidences in school. Faithfully, at 1:22 pm, I'd pull the fire alarm. It was just something that amused me. The principal spoke to me, saying that there was powder on the pull switches; they could put my hand under an ultraviolet light and tell if I was the one who was doing it. I stopped immediately...and likely proved to him that he had caught the right person.

**Senoir Class Picture**

Because the rage in me was so strong, I wanted to fight the world. By this time, my reputation was known as a bully in high school. I felt that, at long last, I had power. Even in the alarm incidences, I proved that I had power, because everyone had to leave the school— I had made it happen.

Was I looking for attention? Probably so...and I was getting it. Not understanding at the time, it was a big cry for help.

To my surprise, in my senior year book, a friend, Dennis wrote, "To the happiest girl in the world."

Years later, at a class reunion, I asked Dennis why he wrote that. He said that I always had a smile on my face and seemed to be so happy. I proceeded to tell him what happened behind closed doors when I left the school. He was shocked, and shared that he, too, had been going through similar treatment during high school.

I had been at his home many times; his family seemed to be happy and lived in a nice home that was spotless. Who would have ever guessed that he was going through the same type of treatment? The truth was that Dennis, himself, always had a smile on his face, during high school that lit up a room. Apparently neither of us wanted anyone to know what we faced when we went home.

◊◊◊

In addition to Gail's personal story, we are also reading about the action—or inaction—of adults during the 1950s. It was a time period in which people looked the other way, and did not question or interfere in another family's business...even when they suspected that a child was being abused.

28

I was told during the mid-1980s that we would be going into a time when *all the secrets would need to come out.* This was told to me by a couple of astrologers. Since I am not an astrologer, my limited understanding is that in the mid-80s Pluto went into Scorpio. Pluto brings up residue in the unconscious and brings "death to the old way of life." Neptune went into Capricorn around the same time. Capricorn represents structures, traditions and foundation, and Neptune is the "great illusion," highly spiritual energy that brings the old illusions to our awareness for spiritual expansion. Saturn was in Scorpio which rules sexuality, and perversions around sexuality. Saturn brings structure to the secrets.

My policy is to listen, take it in, and wait to see if such statements materialize in a grounded way that I am able to recognize. It seemed to have been true. During the mid- and late 1980s and into the 90s, there were an enormous number of adults who began to speak up about memories they had kept inside all their lives. There were others who had spontaneous memories rise about sexual abuse they had experienced during childhood and buried in their unconscious. The time period of the 1940s and 50s were over and such family secrets were no longer being hushed or ignored.

# Learning about Love

I often tell clients that we draw into our lives a mate or partner who reflects what is going on with us at an unconscious level. Like energy attracts like energy. Gail needed to *run away* from her home situation; she drew into her life a man who was *running away* from his parole. He eventually would run away from parental obligations, as well. Eventually he and Gail divorced.

As some single mothers experience, Gail's relationship with her children became strained. She couldn't be there for them while working 12-14 hour days, and had to call upon her parents to assist, which they did.

◊◊◊

## Unusual Circumstances around Marriage and Birth of Children

Out of high school, I was still living at home. My goal had been to become a model. Barbizan Modeling School was scouting me, but because of the turmoil in my family life, my dream never occurred. Instead, I ran away three times, the third time never going back. I was tired of getting accused of things I hadn't done.

I got engaged to someone and that didn't last long, but he lived with the man, Vinnie, who I ended up marrying. Before marriage, I ended up pregnant with Vinnie's child. Life didn't get any easier. I did get married under unusual circumstances.

I didn't know that my husband-to-be had run-ins with the law. One day there was a knock at the door. A man identified himself as Mr. Mozlak, Vinnie's federal probation officer. I invited him in and asked what the problem was; I was not aware of any trouble that Vinnie had with the law. He told me that he was charged with conspiracy against the United States due to possession and passing counterfeit money. Around this time, Vinnie arrived home with a look of shock on his face. I asked him if there was something that he forgot to tell me.

Mr. Mozlak made us both aware that since we were not married, Vinnie was violating his parole. (Back in the late 60s, cohabitating without marriage was a violation). So we had two choices; either he was to leave or we had to get married. Being pregnant, I chose marriage, knowing at the time that it wasn't going to work. But where was I going to go?

I delivered our son, Vincent, in December, 1969. He was truly a gift. My husband and I were happy with this new addition to the family. Still, Vinnie had some underlying things that he continued to withhold. I stuck it out, but things didn't seem to get any better.

On Christmas Eve, 1971, I got a phone call from my doctor's office congratulating me because I was once again pregnant. This was a shock to me; it was not planned. In August 1972, our daughter arrived. I was very upset that it was a girl. I did not hold or feed her, not wanting to bond in any way. The hospital fed her.

When the time came to be discharged, they needed the baby's name. I told them it was "James Joseph." They reminded me that she was a girl. I insisted that her name would be James Joseph. Since I did have to come up with a new name, Vinnie and I talked and came up with the name Kim Marie.

I did have two beautiful children and, as is often said, I wouldn't have given them up for all the money in the world.

By 1974, my husband and I had separated. There were many reasons, including an interfering mother-in-law and his addiction to pornography. Once again, I was struggling alone, this time, raising two children.

Vinnie paid a weekly support of $40 for two children plus the mortgage. I needed to get a job, so I applied for a school bus license. I moved back into the house with my parents and paid $20 a week out of $47 that I took home from the school bus job. My father was never aware that my mother required that payment from me. Finally, I did tell him that I was paying nearly half my weekly income for rent; he got angry and made her pay me back. (Later, when my brother moved back into their house with his wife, both with good-paying jobs, my mother didn't ask them for a dime).

When I got a lawyer, he said, "Vinnie is in the house; you have two small children. We will get him out." I was able to move back into my home and my divorce came through in 1976.

**Driving Commuter Bus**

My Ex-husband decided to buy an airplane, and no longer supported his children. I did allow him to have visitation with his kids because, after all, he was their father. On one of these visits, my son came home and told me their father took them to the airport where he had his plane, but left them on the ground playing while he was in the air with his girl-friend. I didn't say anything to Vinnie, but at his next visitation, I paid a visit to the airport. There were my children, on the ground, age 6 and 4-1/2 supervising the girlfriend's Down syndrome child. This was occurring while their father was flying with his girlfriend. Needless to say, I stopped all visitations.

Vinnie never paid support or the mortgage again, so it became even harder for me. I graduated from a school bus to a commuter bus line, which I worked 12-14 hours a day. Luckily, I got tips on some of these charters because I never would have been able to survive on the $127 to $147 take-home pay. I look back now and don't know how I survived.

◊◊◊

Our souls, I believe, are ever so slowly growing and evolving towards a higher vibration; we often refer to that higher vibration as "Love" or "Light." It seems that, in order to evolve in consciousness, we go through life experiences...to learn. I have often said that in order to learn what love is—a higher form of love—we must also learn what "not love" is. We don't learn through couches and chairs; we learn about love through relationships. It is true for every one of us...and we learn in various ways throughout our lives.

Gail's early life was lacking in love, other than the love she felt from her father. Of course, when we consider her mother's abusive actions towards her, it becomes clear that her mother lacked love in her own life. Therefore, how could her mother give what she did not have? We cannot give to another person what we do not have inside of us; it is impossible.

In addition to our genes, we pass on our unconscious thoughts, beliefs, programming, and emotional energy to our children. Even though she didn't understand it at the time, Gail didn't want anything to do with her daughter when she was born—she refused to accept that her baby was a female. In so doing, her daughter absorbed the anger and resentment that continues to be passed on...from generation to generation.

The good news is that we have the opportunity to heal and to transform our ability to love. Over time, through two men who Gail refers to as the "loves of my life," she begins to experience loving relationships.

◊◊◊

## The Loves of My Life

### Jack

Around the time that I worked for the commuter bus company, I met someone special who came into my life. A friend called me at midnight, telling me that her car broke down on the highway near me. I went to see if I could help her and I was looking under the hood of her car when a state trooper pulled up behind her. Jack approached her vehicle, gave me a snide look, and asked what I was doing. I told him that she had flooded the carburetor by trying to start it too often. He asked, "Are you a mechanic?"

I showed him the butterfly (mechanism) that was in the carburetor, which was stuck. It would not allow the car to start and flooded the carburetor. It was something that my Dad had taught me. Even though Jack knew that I was right, he couldn't imagine me under the hood of the car. He told my friend, Sandy, to get in the police car with him while he called for tow service and wrote out a report. I stood on the sidewalk and noticed that he kept staring at me. He motioned for me to come towards the police car, and told me to get in the back seat. As he was writing the report, Jack kept looking at me in the rear view mirror, not saying anything.

The tow truck came, took Sandy's car, and I took Sandy home with me. She lived a distance, and I didn't want to drive her home. A friend who was a bus driver was out of town and I had the keys to his car. I told her that she could use his car, but she had to have it back by Sunday. I drove her to my friend's car, which was located at the bus company.

I noticed that we passed the same state trooper and he obviously recognized my car. He followed as I pulled into the bus company lot and pulled in behind me, asking what we were doing. I explained that I was letting Sandy use a friend's car. Jack asked me if my friend knew that I was letting someone use his car. I replied honestly, no; he then stated that I was actually stealing a vehicle.

After we bickered back and forth, he allowed Sandy to take the car and continued a conversation with me. He asked me where I worked; I refused to give him any information about myself. He leaned in the car and kissed me on the cheek. I told him that I'd advise his supervisor of what he had just done. He then allowed me to leave and two days later I got a call. Jack had apparently run my license plate number through the system and got my phone number.

The fact that Jack was so persistent raised my curiosity. I hadn't been dating but his beautiful blue eyes and smile made me melt. I knew that he was a *pussy cat* beneath the tough exterior.

On our first date, Jack sat across the table looking into my eyes. He gleamed and kept looking at me, smiling. I asked him what he saw, and he replied, "a beautiful girl." As I knew well, men can say anything to make a woman feel good, so I wasn't buying it. As the night went on we talked about ourselves and I felt there was something about this man I wanted to get to know better.

He said he would like to see me again and I agreed. As I got to know Jack, he was a funny guy. I had such nice times with him. There wasn't a day that went by that I didn't hear from him. I felt joy in his voice and knew this was going to turn out to be something special. We had some things in common; he liked animals and had some show horses, chickens, and later on got a pig as a joke from his cousin. This was a baby pig that weighed about 5 lbs., but later became so big (600 lbs) that he had to give it away to a farm.

We both loved being outdoors, especially going to the beach.

He took me and my kids camping one weekend to Cape May. It was our first time camping trip and it rained all weekend. Thank God my father gave us his pick up truck to go with because it had a cap on the back which kept us from getting soaked. All four of us had to squeeze into the back and try to get comfortable. It was a night I won't forget. Jack snored throughout the whole night keeping me and my kids up.

This was a new experience for us. Since we had never gone camping before; we were roughing it. The next morning it was damp and wet but not raining. Jack cooked breakfast in what little cooking utensils we had. It was a great breakfast; even the kids enjoyed it. The next day we drove into Wildwood so the kids could go onto the boardwalk. We tried to salvage some of the trip. All in all we had a good time with the experience of camping in the rain.

As time went on, we began to fall in love, and it felt so good for me. We became inseparable. When he worked two-day shifts (16 hour shifts for 2 days at a time), I couldn't wait for him to come to see me. It was a longing we both had during those times of being away from each other for two days straight. We spoke on the phone but I wanted to hold him in my arms. Our love was becoming stronger. Jack became my *knight in shining armor.*

This man accepted my children and did a lot of things with them. Since they hadn't seen their father in years, my kids loved him. My father, also, loved this guy. He wanted to see me happy and he saw that when I was with Jack. My dad idolized him.

One day Jack was on duty and came to pick me up in the State Police car. He drove over to my father's house so he could have the police car sit in his driveway. Silly as it sounds, my father was like a child in a toy store when we called him out to the driveway and he saw the car there. Jack told him "Go ahead sit in it, play with the sirens, lights, and get it out of your system." We all laughed to see my father sitting in that car all a-glow. It was a "Kodak moment." I am sorry that we didn't think to take a picture.

There were times when Jack had what they called sub-patrol; when he wasn't working his regular duty he could get overtime. When he was patrolling my area, he called me and I'd ride with him. I sat in the car, watched how radar worked, and learned that it can have false readings. For example, when the wind kicks up and a tree sways, it can give a false reading. So, if someone is driving the speed limit on the road and it is windy and a tree sways, if that person is in line with the tree, he may get a ticket.

Jack realized that the tickets he gave out were expensive to the receivers. Now the prices of tickets have sky rocketed. In addition, he loved nature. He used to say to me," I won't give out a hunk of wood" (meaning that tickets were made from paper—trees). He really thought about saving the trees so most of the time he gave out warnings; such a nice guy. What I loved most about him was that he always gave breaks, but if you gave him a hard time you got a "hunk of wood."

As time went on we did a lot of traveling together. I really started to open my heart and allow love to come in.

Jack came into my life when I was diagnosed with cervical cancer. That was a rough time for me with the pain and not knowing what was going to happen.

The day after surgery, my doctor sat by my side explaining what he found when he opened me up. He said he had never seen anything like it in 30 years of his practice; it was "like a war zone in there." He began to draw me a picture of a varicose vein that was inter- twined around my fallopian tubes and actually strangling them. He said most of the pain was coming from that. Also my appendix was completely gone, disintegrated. I had a prolapsed bladder, endome- triosis and he had to take the cervix because it had a lot of lesions and tumors on it.

His diagnosis was cervical cancer and he said he would wait for the lab to come back with the results, but he knew it had spread fast. I asked him if there a time limit and his face saddened. This doctor had delivered my son when I was 19 and now, 12 years later at age 31, he responded with tears in his eyes. "Gail I would hope you have more time than I think, but right now we are looking at 6 months." It was like a bomb had been dropped on me. I was frozen and stunned; I couldn't move, couldn't think.

That night, Jack came in and I was able to cry to him. We both cried. He softly shared, "How can God take away something so good for me, when I finally found someone who can understand me, and give me love." He said that I had given him the best years of his life. When he held me in his arms I felt like a little child again...this time I was being embraced with Jack's love. This was one time I truly felt the love between us. It was something I never wanted to let go of; it had to be forever. We both cried ourselves to sleep in each other's arms.

The following day I woke up and tried to process all of it. *Did I hear right? Did I hear what my doctor told me? Was this a dream that maybe I was waking from?* I again prayed and prayed hard. As I spoke with God I told him I was needed here for my children, that their father would not be best to raise them. I knew that my mother and father were getting older, and I had to be here for my kids. I said to God, "If you give me one more chance, I will do whatever it is I have to do to stay here...but please give me my health back. My kids need me."

Jack always called me "Bubblie." He said I was full of life and when I smiled (which wasn't often) I lit up a room and lit up his heart. The next day when he called me from work, I answered the phone from my hospital room. He said, "Is this Bubblie?" I smiled and I am sure he could visualize it. I said, "Yes, and I will always keep that smile for you." I told Jack that I talked to God about staying here, and that I was not going anywhere...that I wanted to be with my children and him, and I couldn't leave now.

I was in the hospital for 10 days and when it was time to leave, my doctor sat down with my parents and my children. He told my kids, that "mom" was going to need help and that I was not allowed to do any house work. He said that I needed as much rest as I could get and that they had to be my helpers. Well that was nice, but he created a monster in my son. When we got home my son was barking out orders to my daughter and what she had to do for her chores. It was kind of cute, but Vincent really took on the male role of the home. I didn't want him to carry such a burden worrying about me; I always reassured them I would be okay.

The day came, however, that I had to sit them both down and explain what was happening to me. This was very tough. I tried not to show any emotion because I didn't want them to have any fear of losing me. As I explained what the operation was about, I told them that mommy was very sick and it was going to be awhile before I got any better. I wanted them to know we would all be okay, but if in case anything ever happened to me, they had to help each other. I told them they had to learn to be responsible and help around the house. I also mentioned that as they grew up they had to realize that their grandmother or grandfather would not be around forever so it was important that they got along.

As time went on, I had to go for chemotherapy. I thought, *If this is what I have to do, to sacrifice to be here, then so be it.* I went through seven months of chemo; towards the end my doctor got reports from the radiologist that I was showing no more cancer.

During the time that I went through all this treatment, I also worked my full time job, being sick, passing out, but I had to do it to keep a roof over our heads and food in my kids' mouths. We had many struggles but thank God for my bosses because they were very understanding. They were astonished that I had the strength to go through all that I did.

Jack was by my side every step of the way. We cried together almost everyday but without him being in my life, I truly don't know if I would have gotten through it all. His love was never ending.

A few months later I started to feel nauseous again and I began to wonder and worry that the cancer was coming back. I called the doctor and told him what I was feeling. He told me to come in and they would run some blood work.

After all the chemo that I had gone through and survived, about 9 months later I had a dream of a baby's room. In the dream I was on the porch where I grew up in Jersey City and talked to the spirit world. It was so beautifully set up and someone I worked with was in the dream showing me this room. I woke up thinking, *wow that was strange.*

The next day at work a guy in the next department came over to me and said, "Are you pregnant?" I looked at Ron and said, "Are you crazy? No way." That afternoon the doctor's office called me at work. Dr. Massell asked, "Gail are you sitting down?" I thought, *Oh my God the cancer is back.* Then the doctor told me the tests showed I was pregnant.

What a shock that was! After all I had been through, with the scarring in my fallopian tubes, the lesions, and so much more, how could this be? I certainly didn't think I could have children after all that. He wanted to see me right away. I called Jack and told him the news. We were both in utter shock. We made the appointment with Dr. Massell and sat with him asking how this could have happened. He was startled himself, explaining with all the scarring I had, he couldn't answer. Then, the bad news came.

He told Jack and me that this pregnancy would never reach full term, and if it did I could possibly lose my life. He said with all the chemo and scarring that the chances of the baby being born without any disabilities would be a miracle. I asked what he was trying to tell us. He said I should seriously consider aborting. Once again a bomb had been dropped on me. I didn't believe in abortions. I just sat there and cried. Jack was stunned.

I asked the doctor when an absolute decision had to be made, and if I chose not to abort what were the chances for me or the baby. He stated either I could lose my life or the baby would be deformed. He also said that I would have to think about taking the rest of my life to care for the child. He mentioned that the baby may not live full term. I had to make a decision. The doctor told me to go home and think about it and give him an answer in three days.

I cried all the way home, Jack holding my hand as he drove, saying it would all be okay. When we got home I was once again in his arms, crying saying to myself, *God gave me life and now has given me another life; how can I take this child away?* Was I being tested? Still, I do not in my heart believe God tests us, we test ourselves. So now I had to make the decision.

## Abortion

Jack got on his knees holding my hands and whispered, "Bubblie, you mean the world to me, I can't stand the thought of possibly losing you again. Listen to what the doctor has told you. I do believe God gave you back your life. How this happened, I don't know but we have to come together in thoughts and do what's right for you." He also said that if I chose to keep the child, he would stand by me and help me with raising it.

I talked to God again saying if I went ahead with an abortion, I know He would understand that this is not something I normally would have done...but based on what my doctor was telling me I felt I had to do it. I asked for his forgiveness.

Having made the decision, the day came. Fearful and not knowing what to expect, Jack and I went together; I cried all the way. He tried to comfort me saying, which I agree to be true, "All things happen for a reason."

As we arrived in the parking lot, I couldn't get out of the car. I was frozen, not knowing what to expect. I wished that Jack could be in the room with me, holding my hand, to help me get through it. The nurse sat us down to explain the process. After looking at my records, she agreed that this was something that had to be done.

I was in a pre-surgical room as they prepped me. The nurse explained that the doctor would put a needle into my vagina; she warned me that I would feel it. It would bring on cramps similar to labor pains. I felt so overwhelmed.

I had to be awake during the surgery. I couldn't really feel any pain, although I sensed and heard a suction process taking place. When I turned my head to the left, I saw a canister, which I knew was the beginning fetus, which had just been removed. I wish I had never looked that direction. My emotional feeling—in spite of knowing that the soul was not there—was that I had taken a life.

I was wheeled back into the recovery room, still experiencing pain with cramping and feelings of labor. I lay there, crying and asking for forgiveness.

Still in the recovery room, I noticed a young girl on the stretcher next to me, sitting up, almost in a yoga position with her legs crossed. I asked, "Aren't you in any pain?" Her response to me was, "No, this is my 8th time." I felt at that moment, if I could have gotten off my stretcher, I would have strangled her. How could someone have such disregard for life?

◊◊◊

The issue of abortion has been brought to such extremes in the media as to be termed "for" or "against." As Gail shares, her experience—and that of many other women—is so much more involved, so much more complicated than simple slogans imply.

I'm sometimes asked when the soul enters the body. As with most questions related to spirit, the answer is not the same for everyone. In my experience with regression therapy, it appears that some souls enter the fetus at the moment of birth. Other souls go in and out of the body during the first few weeks after birth. Some souls indicate that they are around the energy fields of the mother and father from the moment of conception. With an abortion, the soul *is not destroyed.* The developing fetus—the physical shell—is what is removed.

Intent is what is important. What is the intent of the birth mother and birth father related to the pregnancy and potential new life? Is there respect for all concerned? As Gail describes—and I emphatically agree—abortion is not an appropriate form of birth control. It shows a disregard for human life.

In most circumstances, making the decision to have an abortion is extremely difficult, and one which the woman will never forget as long as she lives. Aside from physical pain, there may be enormous mental and emotional pain that lasts.

In some instances, the decision is clear, based upon the condition of the mother and/or fetus. No one has the right to ever judge another woman's decisions around such a traumatic and soul searching event.

◊◊◊

As time went on, Jack and I went our separate ways. People come into our life for a reason...and when we close one door, another opens.

## Al

My father crossed over January 12, 1986 and that same year in August I met a man named Al. I should say that I knew him from driving the buses; he too was a bus driver. Everyday when I went to get my bus from the lot in New York, he would be there. Al watched over all the buses in the lot during the day as a security against vandalism.

In August that year Al and I started to talk more often. During that time, I had to go to the lot and pick up a bus, drive to Port

Authority to pick up commuters and take them back to Jersey. I did that for years while still working at the prison at night.

One day Al stood in the stairwell of the bus as I was preparing to leave for Port Authority. As I approached the end of the street where he had to jump off, he surprised me with a kiss on the cheek. He then jumped off the bus and I was in shock. I wondered, *Where did that come from?* I had known him for years, just to pass each other saying hello and now out of nowhere he kissed me on my cheek. After that took place, I felt my father's spirit on the bus with me, but nothing was said.

The next day came and again I had to get my bus in the lot in New York and of course Al was there. I asked him why he kissed me, and he really didn't give me an answer. I think in a matter of a few weeks, we had a date.

I enjoyed being with him and as time went on we grew closer. I could see in his eyes he was falling in love fast. I could see the gleam in his eyes, and my words to him were "There will be no falling in love." I wasn't ready for that after just losing my father. I felt like I had just lost the love of my life in losing him.

I also forewarned Al that I could be a "bitch." He couldn't believe that in me, saying that I was such a beautiful person and willing to help anyone. However, I knew myself. Being a Scorpio and tough because of all I went through in life, I sometimes had to be a bitch to get through things, not necessarily to get my way, just being a bully. Before long, he moved in with me and then I started to fall deeply in love. I knew I was in trouble.

Al and I, like my previous relationship with Jack, became inseparable. We did charters together and traveled a lot on vacations. We frequented the Bahamas often and I really enjoyed each time we went away. I look back now and think that at the time he came into my life I had just lost my father and 2 years later would lose my sister. Al, I believe lost a brother to cancer, so he understood what I was going through.

Al was with me during my times of illness and gave me great strength to get through so many things. I also had to have surgery for a shattered elbow from a prisoner backing me up into a solid brick wall. During that time of recovery, with a cast on my right arm, I couldn't do much. Al was there taking care of me each step of the way, bathing me (I couldn't believe he would do that for me) and feeding me so I could eat. These were things my mother never did for me when I was sick. The love we shared was incredible.

When Al did tours with the buses he would be gone 2 weeks and come back for 3 days and go out again. He worked hard to put his children through college. I had so much respect for him for that. I valued it because my husband never supported our children; I would never have interfered with his duties as a father. So it was hard on both of us to be away from each other but I understood.

There were many times that when Al had to work and I had time off I would go with him on his jobs, such as to Atlantic City. When we got there it would be late at night so all we did was sleep on the bus, but we were together; that's all that mattered. Then there was a time when he had to take a baseball team to North Carolina. He wanted me to go with him because he worked all day and now had to drive at night. So I drove the bus from Newark, NJ to Richmond, VA.

I stopped for breakfast and when he realized that I was stopping the bus, he woke up and asked where we were. I told him we were in Richmond, VA. The person in charge of this trip said to Al, "Man this lady can drive a bus. She went through speed traps and no one came to get her; I'll ride with her anytime." When we left Newark, NJ it was around 1:00 am and when I pulled into the rest area it was close to 6:00 am. I made it in almost 5 hours. Yes, I had the *pedal to the metal*.

Al and I had many trials and tribulations throughout the relationship, but the love we shared was like none other. I never wanted to be away from him and he also felt the same. I always thought if I would ever remarry, he would be the one. This man taught me so many things about life. Being from the South, he came from a big family and had lost his mother and father at a young age. His sister Louise had to pretty much raise the siblings. And through his lessons in life that he shared, I gained much knowledge about survival.

As I sit writing this book, I can say that I feel that Al and I were in a past life together. I sometimes got visions that he was taken away from me. I would see him being dragged away, reaching out his arm as if to cry out for me to help him. In the past life vision, I felt my life would have been in danger so I couldn't help him. I often wonder what I was afraid of—is it that I couldn't accept love from him then...and now I was learning to receive the love that he gave?

I can say today that the love I still carry for him is unreal. There is a connection in the soul and it is hard to let go. I wonder what lesson I was supposed to learn this time around. Al and I broke our relationship 15 years ago; it was one of the saddest times in my life. It hurt so deeply; I felt crushed once again.

I always meditate on New Year's Eve and during that meditation in 2003 I thanked God for all he had given me throughout the year. I had not dated much since the breakup with Al 14 years ago; I was too busy with work. But I felt it was time to ask God and the Universe to send someone into my life, someone who would understand what I do and who I am, someone to love me.

I found out God has a sense of humor. Guess what? Al called. He called 2 weeks after I asked and yet another lesson was learned: *watch what you ask for.* He asked me out to dinner and we reminisced about old times and we had many laughs. As I have always told him the good memories out-weigh the bad, and I always remember the good times. He agreed.

It was about 2 or 3 days later that I got another call from Al. He said he wanted to ask me a question. I said, "What is it?" Al replied "If I asked you to marry me, would you?" Well that was a loaded question, but how could I answer that after not being with him for 14 years? I mentioned to him how much I have changed. During the time we were together, my psychic ability had been put on hold. Even though I could feel his energy and his not believing that I had changed, I stated that we would have to basically start all over again and that would be a time process.

Al asked if I still loved him and I said I would always love him because of the soul connection I always felt towards him. He told me that he still loves me and always will.

So I was stuck in my heart once again. I allowed the doors to be opened and wasn't sure if this was a good thing. I didn't want to get hurt again by it not working out. I prayed so hard to God and asked him to show me the way. We stayed in touch, went out a few times and I could see my heart was opening wider and wider to let him in. Then the games began. He called and said he didn't think this was going to work. Bam! I felt like I'd had a knock out from him. I was so mad at myself for letting my heart open once again, but I had no one to blame but myself.

We went back and forth; it was like he was dangling a carrot in front of me and stupid me went for it. I finally asked Al if he was getting back at me for my hurting him in the past. He said "no" and questioned how I could say that, but that is what I felt like I was going through. I had to be strong each time he called. When I answered the phone, I asked God to give me strength. I started questioning myself—was I lonely and wanted him back? I got the answer so strong from my guides "No."

Grey Wolf stepped in and said to me *You knew this hadn't ended in your heart. This had to occur to find yourself and see where you were going on your journey. You had to seek the truth and not allow anyone or anything to get in your way. You had to feel the pain to make yourself even stronger, for what you have gone through in life. This will be your teaching for those around you.*

Well I pondered what Grey Wolf said to me and certainly understood. No matter what I have gone through in this lifetime, I somehow did get the strength to get through it. I am very proud of myself when I think of it. I really didn't need a man to be in my life. God was always there showing the way.

I asked Grey Wolf if this relationship with Al was now completed. *No there is more to come, but you will be shown in many ways the love that you both have shared and will always keep close to your heart.* Of course I said to Grey Wolf that wasn't what I wanted to hear. I couldn't imagine what was going to be next.

It was slowly being shown to me, that when I called Al, I could pick up in his energy that he was very confused. He didn't know what he was looking for. He was now with a woman that he left me for and I knew he was not happy in his heart. He has to look for answers and I don't think he will find them anytime soon.

As time went on I was being shown more truth. As I talked to Al, I mentioned that I saw he hadn't changed; it doesn't take long to see things. Yet he always threw in my face that I hadn't changed. I reminded him that he hadn't spent enough time with me to find out, but that was okay. I know in my heart that I will always love him, but it would not work if we tried to start over again. I often asked him what his fears were; I could sense a fear he was holding onto. I said to myself *how funny it is no matter how old we are we still carry fears.*

When I asked him if he could help me paint my kitchen ceiling, he said yes. I will say that no matter what I asked him for he was there to help me. He chose to come on Father's day to paint. I knew his children lived in the Carolina's so it wasn't that he would be spending time with them, but again that was his choice.

When he arrived, I saw him pull up outside my house and then my phone rang. I said to myself, *If that is him I will be mad.* Why? Because Al saw a car parked in front of my house and thought I had a man with me. His suspicion (jealousy) had been a pattern of the past and once again I saw the "old Al" coming out.

When I answered the phone I blurted out, "Do not tell me you are calling to see if I have someone in the house with me, because if I were to have a man here I certainly wouldn't have you come to help me!" I was upset yet God showed me again that Al hadn't changed. *Why in Sam Hill* would I ask him to help me if I had someone else here...so the frustration began. I was so glad this took place because I can't handle the stress of petty things; life is too short.

When he came into the house Al wanted a glass of milk. I told him I would go to the corner store and get fresh milk. As I was driving to the store I noticed a man on the lawn face down, and wondered, *Is that guy okay?* On the drive back I saw this man still on the grass face down and I didn't like what I was getting.

It was June and close to graduation time. Some kids like to put dummies on the streets and lawns to make people think it is a real person, so I had to turn around to make sure it wasn't a dummy. It wasn't. When I got back home I said to Al, "I just saw a man lying on the lawn face down with a red baseball cap on." Al said he saw the same man when he came onto that street. I asked why he hadn't said anything to me; I was going to call the police to report it. I didn't know if he was okay. (I know I am psychic but we don't know everything).

Al responded, "Well, he and his old lady must have had a fight and she threw him out and he just slept on the lawn, like you did to me that time." Well there was my answer to his fears. When we were together before, I did ask Al to leave one time but he did not sleep on the lawn. He told me he slept in his car. Obviously, he never forgot that.

So when I had the chance, I cornered him. He was washing the paint brushes out by the kitchen sink. I turned him around to look right into my eyes and asked, "Is that your fear of coming back to me—you think I will ask you to leave again?"

I told him I was now 14 years older and much wiser. I would never do that. In fact in a relationship people have to be able to communicate; that was something we lacked previously. He couldn't look me in the eyes, but I was given my answer about his fears. I knew immediately this was never going to work out even if we tried. We both had a jealousy with each other and no communication. I truly was happy that I learned this. On that day, I knew it would never work.

So he cleaned up and went on his way, but he continued to call. I asked him nicely not to call me again; it really wasn't going to work even though I would always love him. We had a song we shared together, "Always and Forever," and when we spoke we always said that to each other, because our love would always be 'Always and Forever."

Months went by and once again he called me saying he still loved me. I told him as long as he has the fears he carries and still lives with another woman, I could never go back to him. Even though he is not married, I realize that with this woman he can come and go as he pleases. He doesn't have to answer to her. He does what he wants to do and is not afraid to be put out of the house by her. So, he is comfortable where he is at.

The year 2005 arrived and he was still calling. What he didn't realize is that each time I would see him call on my caller ID it would hurt me. Why wouldn't he let go once and for all? That little door would open up in my heart and I had to remind myself, "No this is not good." I'd walk away from the phone. Al never knew the whole story of what I had gone through in life with my mother and family.

I took the draft of the first chapter of my book, printed it out, and called him to meet him on his job. I asked him to read it. It was the beginning of my story and the pain was there, yet I hadn't even touched the iceberg of the story yet. I asked him to call me back with any comments. He did. He felt very bad that I was molested 3 times. He never knew that and I could feel his empathy for me. I wasn't looking for sympathy, but wanted to let him know I had gone through enough pain in my life and didn't want any more from him.

I asked him on January 13, 2005 not to call me again. It was 19 years and one day after my father's death, He promised he wouldn't. I thought *how strange—19 years and one day from my father's death. I felt my father had sent him to me and now we have come to the final ending of this relationship and friendship.* It is over once and for all, so I thought.

One more call came from Al and he said to me—which shocked me because I would never have thought he would think this way— "Gail I feel if it is really meant to be, it will be...maybe not now, but in time. I still love you, Always and Forever." I cried knowing that I finally closed that door, Always and Forever.

◊◊◊

It has been said that if a woman had a good relationship with her father, she unconsciously seeks a similar person. Notice that I've moved that sentence a step away from the well-known statement that *we marry our fathers.*

When we are children, our "world" is our home and family; our sense of love, security and safety in that world is our parents. In Gail's case, her sense of love and safety came only through her father.

Since Gail's father was at sea so much, she missed him...and felt that she needed his help and wanted to be there for him, as well. When she was a child, she said a prayer to God that was answered 30 years later.

## My Father

As a child, I'd often stand looking out the window wondering where my daddy was. I used to write him letters and try to tell him that I was being a good girl, but that my mother was always punishing me and I didn't understand why.

Growing up and seeing a stork carrying a child in a blanket, I thought the little birdie took the letter to my father way out to his ship at sea. My daddy wrote me a letter saying that the little birdie told him that I was being a bad girl. I used to get so mad at that little birdie – why did he lie?

As I shared earlier, one day I looked out to the sky and said to God, "Please let me be there if anything happens to my daddy." The day that he died—30 years later—it turned out that I was the only one there.

My father had a stroke and was in a hospital. My sister called, telling me to meet her and my mother at the hospital at 1:00 pm. I replied that I couldn't get there then, but could probably arrive by 3:00 pm. As it was, I got there at 1:00, sensed something was terribly wrong, looked around the parking lot for my sister's car and could not find it. I went into the hospital and I heard them paging Code Blue 032, which was my father's bed number in his room.

As I entered the hospital, I ran down the hallway to his room and a nurse tried to stop me. I pushed her aside, got into his room and they were working to revive him. As I screamed, "Daddy don't go!" I saw his spirit lifting.

They took me out of the room and tried to convince me that he was going to be okay. I told the nurse, "You're wrong, because I saw him leaving." She must have thought I was nuts. Then I realized that my mother and sister were not there at 1:00 pm, as planned.

I went to the front lobby by the waiting room to see if they were coming; it seemed forever. By the time they got there, it was 3:00 pm, so time reversed itself. They were to be there at 1:00 – I was to be there at 3:00, but I got my wish.

Even though my father couldn't be there for me because of his career, at the end, I was there for him. I was the only one with him when he left. That's when I started to learn to *watch what you ask for.* My child's prayer to God had been answered.

# Turning Points

We all have "turning points" in our lives, those times when something happens and life is forever changed. Discovering that she had cancer was certainly one of those times for Gail. During the surgery, she had a combination of hallucination and near-death experience. The hallucination was the image and feeling of being on a stretcher and going into a river. The near-death experience followed with feeling herself to be out of body and in a most beautiful place that awakened all of her senses to the colors and aromas.

Referring to her hallucination, the river—water—is a symbol of the unconscious mind. Her deeper mind gave her a message that her future would take her into the deeper recesses of her unconscious. This would certainly hold true.

Immediately after the surgery, Gail received the startling message from her doctor that she had approximately 6 months to live. This was a turning point in her life. Facing death, of course, is perhaps the greatest challenge that any of us will face.

Unable to work, she was forced to go within, to pray, and to ask for help, pleading with God to let her live for her children. She also "bargained" with God that she would do whatever he called her to do, if he would show the way.

At the end of the 6 month period, she was still alive...and God did show her the way that she could serve. The first clue came with a psychic who worked with police departments on murder cases. Helen stressed that Gail had psychic gifts that could be used to help others.

It surprises me now to learn that, at that time, Gail thought of psychic abilities as "witchcraft." Even though her communication with the spirit world as a child had been very positive, playing around with a Ouija Board had resulted in negative experiences. She also had a *deep seated fear of* witchcraft which was a soul memory, although she didn't know it at the time. Helen taught Gail about how to use her gift in the "Light" and to help others. It would take a while before Gail began her work in a similar way; however, she kept her word to God.

## Cancer and First Near-Death Experience

During this period of my life, I didn't have any contact with the spirit world. I was focused on survival for me and my children. Nevertheless a re-awakening occurred in 1981 when I went into the hospital for cancer surgery.

My friends from ADT Alarm Company joked with me when they learned that I'd be in the hospital. They asked what time my surgery was and I told them. They said that they would make the fire alarms go off at that time. I just laughed because I knew they really couldn't do that.

While waiting for my parents to come before going into the operating room, Dr. Massell said, "We have to go in. We're all on a tight schedule." I pleaded, "I don't think I'm going to make it; please let me wait until they arrive." Then I heard a nurse's voice telling my parents, "She is in the hallway, ready to go in." My Dad kissed my forehead and I held his hand as he said to the doctor, "Please take care of my baby." Dr. Massell responded, "Your baby? She's been my baby; I've been taking care of her for a long time and nothing is going to happen." They whisked me away.

In the operating room and going under anesthesia, the fire alarm started to go off. I heard Dr. Massell say, "Someone make a phone call. Is this the real thing, or is it a test?" When I went under the anesthesia, I had a dream/fantasy that they were evacuating the hospital. Someone was pushing my stretcher down the hill and let me go. I went right into the river.

Suddenly, I was back in the operating room, out of body, listening to Dr. Massell talk and performing my surgery—not a pretty sight.

Next, I found myself going to the *other side* and seeing people walking to and fro, but not communicating with each other. It was the most wonderful feeling I had ever felt, the flowers were so beautiful and their smell incredible. I especially remember the clean air—nothing like we have here. I got to observe what was going on and then, unfortunately, had to come back.

◊◊◊

The Aramaic [Aramaic is the language that Jesus spoke] word for death translates to *not here, present elsewhere.* It gives us a broader picture—a person who has died is not "gone," s/he is "elsewhere."

A 1997 poll estimated that 15 million Americans have had a near-death experience. Typically, near-death experiencers register neither pulse nor breath for an average of 10 to 15 minutes and it is not unusual to hear of those who were "dead" over an hour.

There are four types of near-death experiences, according to NDE researcher, PMH Atwater:[2]

- Initial experience, which involves elements such as a loving nothingness, brief out-of-body experience, and/or friendly voice.
- Unpleasant and/or hell-like experience, such as an encounter with a threatening void, hellish scenes or hauntings from one's own past.
- Pleasant and/or heaven-like experiences. This includes loving family reunions with spirits, religious figures or light beings.
- Transcendent experiences, such as exposure to other-worldly dimensions and scenes beyond the individual's frame of reference. It sometimes includes revelations of greater truths.

◊◊◊

As mentioned in the chapter with Jack, after the extensive surgery, Dr. Massell told me that it didn't look good. I asked him how much time I had and he said, "I wish that you can have a long life, but we're looking at 6 months."

I prayed so hard to God not to take me because my kids were small and needed me. My son was 12 years old and my daughter was 9. Their father was gone and no one knew where he was, and I didn't want him to step in and raise them knowing he would have led them into some unsavory things.

---

[2] Atwater, P.M.H. with David H. Morgan. *The Complete Idiot's Guide to Near-Death Experiences.* Alpha Books, 2000. [Used with permission]

Before my surgery, I had asked my doctor not to tell my parents what he found; I wanted to know first. I especially didn't want my dad to worry about me.

My parents soon came in. I saw the look on my dad's face as if he knew even though the doctor said he hadn't said anything as per my request. My father kept rubbing my forehead and kissed it. I held back the tears. I wanted to cry so hard but had to be strong for my father. I didn't want him to know he was going to lose his little girl, his baby.

Eventually, I gathered the courage to sit down with my children and explain what was happening. I told them that their grandparents wouldn't be here forever, and mommy was very sick so they had to learn to take care of each other and be responsible. I look back now and realize what a burden I must have put on them at that age. I told my son that he would be the man of the house. I don't know if that was good or bad...he became a "little dictator."

In the next 6-months of recuperation, I had lots of time to think about what I had gone through. I prayed so hard to God. I begged that whatever he wanted me to do, to please show it to me, and I would do it.

## Working with Inmates as a Corrections Officer

I had been out of work for approximately 8 months and was terminated from my job for being away so long. I realized that I couldn't keep going on the salary that I had been making anyway, and started to look for something else.

Jack assisted in getting me a job with the Garden State Parkway. I still drove the busses out of New York late in the afternoon. Because of the long hours, my parents watched my children from Monday through Friday and I had them on Saturday and Sunday. There came a time, while driving the busses—in order to keep my job—that I also had to work on Saturdays and Sundays.

My children were active in sports in elementary school. I felt so awful that, in working such long hours, I could never attend. It was bad enough that they didn't have a father; now they didn't have a mother. They both played soccer and I couldn't attend any of their afternoon games.

My daughter took up music and played the flute; at least I was able to attend her spring and winter concerts. When she was in Brownies and moved up to Girl Scouts, I managed to be there that night because all the other girls would have their mothers with them.

I realized that something had to give with working these two jobs so I searched for a single full-time job. I was able to get one in a retail company as a store security detective and eventually worked my way up to security manager. Unusual at the time, I had very understanding bosses who allowed me to bring my children to the job sites. This was my time to be with them, even though I was also working. At other times, my parents still took care of them.

The job as a store detective gave me an opportunity to teach my children an important lesson about stealing. With the cameras, I showed them that one never knows when they are being watched.

I stayed in the security field for several years until I was approached about becoming a corrections officer. I met with the under sheriff and took a tour of the jail to see what this job would consist of. As I went through the men's quarters, some unsavory things were said to me. It was just a ploy to scare me.

One tough looking inmate called out to me, "Hey Blondie, I got something for you." When I turned around to see, he was holding his penis in his hand. I responded, "That's not big enough for me." This made him, as they called it in the jail, "go off," because I embarrassed him in front of the other inmates. Even though I was frightened at the time, the words were an automatic response from the childhood bully inside of me. I got the job.

Before I could begin working, however, I had to go through a hearing test and 5 hours of psychological tests. One of the questions asked was if I had any lesbian tendencies. Another question was if I had any animals. What surprised me more was the follow up: "Are they possessed?"

I was asked to draw pictures of a house and person who went with the house. I realized that he was looking for a drawing that had details in it, not simply a stick figure in front of a box. I drew a house, a figure, window with curtains, and chimney with smoke coming out, a lamp post, American flag flying, and landscaping around the house. It seemed that he was seeking someone who was detail oriented and observant.

When the examination was completed, he did not say a word to me. I knew that he had to make his determination as to whether I was capable of handling the job and send his report to the county. Once I started working, I learned that the other officers agreed that this man should not have been a psychologist. As it turned out, they eventually replaced him.

The first week of being on the job, I didn't think I was going to make it. The inmates knew that I was the new kid on the block. They put me through hell. I knew that I had to make a tough decision, either to stay on the job or leave. It offered good money and had excellent benefits. I thought of my kids and decided that I had to make it work in order to stay.

On the first day shift that I worked, I was in the kitchen with the inmates while they were eating breakfast. Because I was standing guard, they called me "the mannequin." It was because I was standing so stiff and afraid to move. They kept it up and kept it up. One inmate, named Nissey, who was the leader of that cell block, stood up, slammed her hand on the table, and said, "No one is to harass Officer Lionetti, and if I find out you do, you're mine." They took a liking to me and from that day on, I never had a problem in the female wing.

I learned a lot of *tricks of the trade* through the inmates. I now know how to make wine out of apples and bread. In spite of it all, I have good memories of working at the jail and surprisingly, it wasn't with my fellow officers; it was with the inmates. I learned that the officers would set someone up in a minute and could not be trusted whereas the inmates, once they took a liking to me, I had it made.

I had the midnight shift and often had to continue into the day shift when other officers called in sick. I worked between the female and male quarters, more often on the female side. When I worked the midnight shift, inmates were sleeping.

When 5:00 a.m. came, it was another world. The natives became restless. The inmates didn't talk, they screamed piercingly, even when one was standing right next to them. At any given time, there were up to 180 female inmates and 400 males. It got to the point that when I went home to my children, I talked to them in the same way. My children would ask, "Why are you screaming?" I had to explain what it was like in the jail.

## Facing My Fear of Witchcraft

It seems as if God sent a woman, named Helen, into my life who also was a psychic. I met her under unusual circumstances.

One of my girlfriend's husbands was murdered and the local police called Helen to help with the case. Helen invited me to go with her into New York. The murder had taken place on the piers. We met with the detective who was on the case and I watched as Helen dazzled the detective with her information. We secretly called this detective "the lion." He was one of those cops who come across harsh and crude; he didn't want to believe in psychic ability. Still, after we gave him information, he brought out other cases for us to look at.

When I first met Helen, she asked if I knew how gifted I was. My initial reaction to her was strong, saying, "I don't believe in this stuff and I don't want to deal with it. It's witchcraft." The reason for my outburst was that prior to meeting her, I had been playing with a Ouija Board and got negative influences from it.

Helen proceeded to enlighten me about the good parts of the gift that we both had. She said that using witchcraft can be either good or bad. She explained that one can use the *dark side* of psychic ability, but that I would be using it in the *Light*. After a 3-hour conversation, she had me thinking differently, and invited me to her meditation group. That's when my psychic gifts opened up again.

Six months had passed and I was still alive. After working with Helen and seeing how my gift could be used to help others, I began to realize that God was showing me how my life could be of service. After all, he had kept me here for a reason.

## Second Near-Death Experience

When I had to go to the hospital for my second cancer surgery, I got many cards and letters from inmates. The night before I left, I smuggled in little Whitman's Sampler candy boxes, which would have been considered contraband. I could have lost my job, but I wanted the inmates to know how I appreciated their concern for me. One inmate, Rose, said that she would treasure that empty box after she ate the candy.

Rose, wrote me a letter stating that when they had play time, which consisted of 20 minutes, they were in the courtyard and another inmate, Gagy, called "time out." While all the other officers stood around, Gagy said, "Officer Lionetti is now in surgery, and we will take a moment in prayer for her." I had gained respect from the inmates that other officers didn't have.

> "We actually got just about the whole women's quarters together in prayer about a quarter till 2. How? I guess it was a lot more hearts open to you. Most of the women here, especially me [Rose], Basemah, and Gagy really appreciate an officer who treats you like a woman, and not just a prisoner or a job. The love you pass off as you are here stands out around the rest. You should have seen the face of the officers when Gagy called me and said, "the time." I was along with quite a few others in the middle of a real good volley ball game. Instantly, time out sign was made and announcement and you could have heard a pin drop. Even a male officer returning a ball stood and stared with the rest of your co-workers at this instant silence outside and in. Until the 23rd Psalm was read and they [corrections officers] began to realize it was a prayer for an officer and they knew nothing about it. I was so proud to know you and be a part of (believe it or not) this jail, but mostly proud to be a part of the Lord and your miracle."

> Love-
> Rose

On June 10, 1987, I made my second trip to the hospital for cancer surgery. In the recovery room, I heard the doctor speaking to my son on the phone telling him that I was okay and that everything went well. The next thing I heard was the nurse saying, "Gail, can you hear me?" I answered yes, but she continued to ask, "Gail can you hear me?" She then started to smack my hand and kept calling

"Gail, Gail." I kept answering, "What? I can hear you. What?"...but they couldn't hear me.

Then she started smacking my face, yelling, "Gail, can you hear me?" I got so upset, because I kept replying, "Yes, I can." I became frustrated and started to cry. The tears were coming down the side of my face. Then I heard the doctor yell, "Call respiratory. We're losing her." I said to myself, *I wonder who they are losing.* The next thing that I knew, I was lifting out of my body and went to the "other side."

I did not have the effect of going through a tunnel, but I know that once I went over, my family was there to greet me. My father was there, aunts and uncles who I had forgotten. My Aunt Gladys and Uncle Charlie came towards me. I had forgotten about them since it had been so many years since they had crossed over; I was excited to see them. I reminisced with them about the times they had parties at their house. Even though I had fun, my mother drank and became loud, nasty and obnoxious.

Next, Aunt Mae [see communion photo] came to the forefront with her two sons standing behind her. She wore her little flowered housedress with a full apron and her hair in a bun; she still wore her little black shoes that I remembered so well. I was so excited to see her because, as a child, she sent me a birthday card every year with a $5.00 bill inside. At that time, $5.00 was a lot of money. As a child, I didn't care about the card; I ripped the envelope open just to get the $5.00.

In this heavenly space, however, I made sure that I told her how thankful I was to get her card, even letting her know that I never read the card and just took the money. I'm sure I thanked her when she was on the earth plane, because my mother would have made me do it. But, I really wanted my aunt to know that I truly appreciated her thinking of me every birthday; it meant a lot to me.

As she started to move back from me, Aunt Mae said, "God helps those who help themselves." This statement was something she always said when we used to visit for lunch. We were taught not to dive into the food at someone else's house, no matter how hungry... so my brother and I would just sit and look at the table with food. Aunt Mae would call out, "What are you waiting for? Go ahead and make your sandwich. God helps those who help themselves."

I even saw the animals that we had when we were growing up, including birds, dogs, and cats. After I was greeted by my family, I seemed to be pulled to the left. It brought me into a room that, as I stood alone, I felt a presence that I believe was God with Jesus to the right.

What appeared before me was like a movie screen of my life from the day that I was born until the day that I crossed over (the current day – I was 37 years old). It seemed like a matter of seconds, but I saw things that happened to me as a child, good and bad. It seemed that there was a pause on two events that occurred in my life and I just didn't understand what was being shown to me.

Going back to my angry days in high school, it was shown to me how I had beaten up all these kids. Then it reflected how I did damage to peoples' vehicles by breaking windshields, flattening tires, and putting sugar down tanks. As I stood there, it just seemed that the scenes kept going back and forth, back and forth. I tried to explain to God that the scene of the damage of the vehicles was retaliation for what the people did to me. I wanted to make them pay. Still, the scene kept going back to where I would see me beating these kids and watching them cry. I tried to tell God, "But I had to make them pay."

I realized at that time, that God did not judge me. I stood in judgment of myself. He was an all-loving God. I just didn't understand why he kept showing me the scenes of these children crying. He said that I had to go back. I begged him not to send me back, but to let me stay.

It was so peaceful and tranquil and beautiful over there. Why would I want to go back to that hell?

When I woke up in the hospital, I was in intensive care and on a respirator. I looked around me and saw men in uniforms and wondered why I was in jail. It took me a few minutes before I realized that these were the guys who I had worked with, standing vigil over me. I saw my son, and he asked what happened. I couldn't talk because I was still on the respirator.

In time, they cleared the room and removed the respirator. Within a few minutes my doctor arrived. He asked what happened. I replied, "What do you mean?" He said, "You've been gone for 3 days." In shock and confusion, I asked, "Where did I go?" He responded, "You tell me."

My doctor was well aware of my psychic gifts. He sat next to me and I proceeded to tell him that I had seen him on the phone with my son telling him that everything had gone well. Then I explained how I heard the nurses saying "Gail, can you hear us?"...and becoming very frustrated that they weren't hearing me. I told him that I also heard him saying, "Call respiratory; we're losing her"...and how I wondered to myself who they were losing. My doctor said that at no time did I respond.

I felt comfortable in also telling the doctor that I had seen my deceased relatives on the other side. He was very accepting and in awe of my experience. He knew about my gift and believed in it.

After staying three more days in the hospital, I was discharged and sent home. Since I was not allowed to work, I decided to watch TV. I turned on the Morey Povich Show and the topic was "high school bullies." I listened to grown adults on stage telling their stories, and sobbing over the pain that they endured from bullies when they were in school.

What got me the most was when the bullies entered the stage and were confronted by the people they bullied; they didn't even remember them. It saddened me to see the anguish of these adults crying from the pain that these bullies had instilled in them so long ago.

At that point, I realized that when God was showing me the scenes of children crying, he was trying to make me realize, *you can fix material things...but you cannot fix the pain that you instill on a person.* I sat there and cried. I called upon God and spoke out loud, "Dear God, now I understand what you were trying to show me."

From that time on, my life changed. I tried, and continue to try, to help as many people as I can. Since that near-death experience, it is my interpretation that I was in heaven and this is our hell. Still, my faith always sustains me, no matter what crosses I have to bear.

◊◊◊

Due to today's medical technology, we now have a vast number of people who claim to have had a "near-death experience." Originally termed by Dr. Raymond Moody, the near-death experience, or NDE, is accepted by most people as actual phenomena that a person experienced.

Of course there are skeptics who say that it is not a near-death experience in which the person actually spoke to deceased loves ones, but that it is brain-chemical reaction. Nevertheless, in research studies, it becomes clear that:

- the experience, although subjective, is also supported by medical technology indicating that the person has "died" while on the operating table or in recovery,
- information is sometimes given or perceived from a deceased loved one in which the person could not have gained under ordinary circumstances,
- visual and auditory memories of the medical team's activities to revive the "deceased person" are clear and related from a perspective considered "impossible" for the patient to know.

Although many NDEs refer to a tunnel of *White Light* that guides them, it is not the experience of every person. Gail did not have the tunnel experience. She did, however, meet with deceased relatives, including some that she had forgotten.

A *life review* is another part of the NDE that many experiencers have related. In Gail's life review, she kept being shown two scenes repeatedly: that of her beating up classmates and one of destroying another person's property. Although she kept trying to explain to the Being that she felt was God, that she *had to make them pay*, the scenes kept repeating...as if to focus her spirit/mind on them in order to remember.

Gail refers to sensing God and Jesus. NDE research indicates that most often the spiritual teachers of one's belief system are a part of the experience. This is not always true, however; occasionally a different spiritual teacher may appear, such as the Buddha to a Christian or Mohammad to a child born in a Buddhist culture.

Gail's near-death experience was one that was positive and loving, which is true of the majority of NDEs. Nevertheless, some NDEs have resulted in sensing a dark place or "hellish figure."

Gail's near-death experiences reveal the vast difference between the "soul" and "physical personality." While in that heavenly space, she wanted to stay; she did not want to return to what she called the "hell on earth. " However, once back in her physical body, she pleaded with God to let her live so that she could take care of her children.

# People Come into Your Life for a Reason

As we examine the relationships in our lives, we can acknowledge that they fall into very different categories: brief or long-lasting, positive or negative influences, comforting or challenging, intimate or superficial...and they are all teachers. Whether or not we wish to recognize it, every person in our life is a *reflection* of some aspect of our own nature or personality. And...the person who we most struggle with—the one whose actions or attitude we most dislike— is the one who gives us the greatest opportunity to see ourselves.

People who come into our lives offer us an opportunity to grow and to learn more about love. It may not be apparent in the relationship; however, if we look more deeply, each person has something important to teach us. From the clerk behind the counter to the mechanic who fixes our car to our favorite—or least-favorite— professor to each family member, each person comes into our life for a reason.

◊◊◊

## An Inmate and a Family

While working in the prison I met Barbara (called Gagy), an inmate. She had a very tough exterior and was a person I wouldn't want to meet in a dark alley. She appeared mannish by her actions, was addicted to drugs and alcohol; she was a lesbian, and she had a heart of gold. When she smiled, she lit up the room. She was always running her mouth and getting in trouble in jail, but I knew that deep down inside, there was a soft person.

One day while on watch over a murderer in a segregated cell, they were overcrowded and Gagy was placed in the same cell. I sat in the cell block with Gagy and we engaged in a conversation about families. She told me her dad had passed away; she was still upset that she hadn't been able to go to his funeral because she was in jail. She said she would never want that to happen if, "God forbid anything happened to my mother." She said she loved her family very much, but she f----ed up her life and didn't see them much. She told me she had three sisters and a brother and that her one sister, Ann, always went out of her way to help her.

I told her a little about my own family, that I had two children and the struggles I had in raising them. I shared that I wondered if I was supposed to work in the jail to teach them. From things I had seen go on in the jails, I'd go home and tell them some stories to forewarn them. Knowing what goes on behind the scenes, I told Gagy that I don't know what I would ever do if either of my children went to jail.

For the few hours that we spoke, it taught me that not only Gagy, but the rest of the inmates are simply human. I found myself preaching to the corrections officers (COs) that no matter what the crime, the inmates are only human; we all make mistakes. From that time on, Gagy and I gained a distant but honest friendship.

After my cancer surgery, I had to give up the job as a corrections officer. I began working as a loss prevention manager with K-Mart. I became friends with one of the supervisors on the floor. One day in a phone conversation I talked about working at the jail. After I talked about one of the inmates, Gagy, I heard a silence on the other end. I asked Ann Marie why she became so quiet.

She responded, "Gagy is my sister." I almost dropped the phone. How could it be that I took care of her sister in the jail, remembered the conversations we had about her family, and now was working with Gagy's sister. I thought to myself, *How can this be?* Yet, I do not believe in coincidences.

Ann Marie and I had such a connection that I felt she was like a sister to me. I got to meet her family, including her mother. I told them all about Gagy and how she missed her family and that she really did feel bad for what she had put them through

Ann Marie had a son named Chip who worked with us in K-Mart. I loved his smile and I used to play pranks on him in the store. He eventually found out it was me because at my 40th birthday party, Chip got up and teased about how I used to call the outside phone and pretend I was a shopper who was attracted to him. In the "birthday roast," he teased about how I breathed heavily into the phone and said that I loved his "tiny hiney." Two weeks after that party, Chip was killed in a car accident. It was a day that I will never forget. I asked how I could help the family and they wanted me to find Gagy, which I did. Now, I was there for Ann Marie.

As the friendship grew, I told Ann Marie about my life with my mother. It seemed that I grew closer to Ann Marie's mother, Delores, as well. As I got closer to Delores, I started to call her "mom."

Eight months later, "mom" (Delores) called me up to have dinner with her. When I walked into the house, she was in the kitchen with her arm behind her back. I asked what she was up to. She, too, knew of the problems with my mother. She brought her arm in front of her body holding a red rose, saying, "You're like a daughter to me. I've adopted you as my daughter." We both hugged and cried. When I got back to my job, an hour later I received a phone call from my daughter telling me that my mother had passed away. I thought to myself, *How strange; I just got a new mother and lost the one I was born to.* Coincidence? I think not.

I got a call from "mom" (Delores) two months later saying that Gagy wanted to see me. When I got to her house, I was shocked at the way Gagy looked. She wore a scarf on her head, had lost all her teeth and looked very frail. She proceeded to tell me that she had AIDS. She wanted to thank me for all I had done for her and her family.

I asked Gagy if she had it all to do over again if she would have changed her lifestyle; she said no. I thought to myself, *She already went to hell and back. Why would she choose this again?* But I realize that it was the only lifestyle she knew.

A month later, I was vacationing in Florida and heard Gagy's voice, saying goodbye to me. When I returned home, there was a message from her mother saying that Gagy had passed over.

Only a year later, I visited "mom" (Delores) in the hospital; she was suffering from Lou Gehrig's disease. I was stunned by the way that she looked. We had a visit together with lots of laughs and two months later she joined her grandson and her daughter. In spite of understanding that her spirit was with them, it was a very sad day in my life.

So, from the time I worked at the jail, for 5 years this family had become a part of my life and I was a part of theirs. I then began to realize that nothing is ever a coincidence. People do come into your life for a reason. We can help each other and when it's time to move on, God sets us on another path.

## Trip Back to Home and School

I heard about a man named Ray in Jersey City, where I grew up, who had Stigmata (bleeding from the hands and/or feet similar to that of Jesus). He was known to have the Blessed Mother's spirit visit in his home. I decided to go with a few friends to check this out. In Ray's home he had a picture of St. Ann, along with the Blessed Mother. The picture actually showed oils coming from the eyes of St. Ann (mother of the Blessed Mother); she was crying oils. When I saw the picture weeping oils, the hair actually stood up on my body. I definitely felt the presence of something incredible; it was a very spiritual evening for me.

I sat at a table with Ray and about 25 people in the room saying the Rosary together. That night was pretty amazing with what I had experienced through the picture and the energies in the room praying the Rosary.

After saying prayers, I noticed a man sitting next to me whom I did not know. A spirit came to me and said he belonged to this man. No matter where I go spirits follow. I asked the spirit who he was and he replied, "Robert." I had to think how I would approach this; the man had never met me and no one in the room knew what I did.

I leaned over and asked if he knew a Robert. He looked at me and then I introduced myself. He introduced himself as Wayne Roesch and his wife next to him as Toni. He couldn't figure out who Robert was, so I explained he was in spirit and told him of my psychic gifts.

A few weeks later, I went to a Christmas Rosary at a hall in Jersey City where every year they play out the birth of Jesus. I noticed Wayne and his wife in the back of the room.

At the Christmas Rosary they had a duplicate copy of the picture of St. Ann which Ray had donated; they were raffling it off. I figured it was going to a good cause and I'd contribute. From the raffle, Ray would donate to those in need, as he often did through the *Ray of Hope Foundation*.

In October, 2002 I had been awarded some monies from a compensation case. While I sat in the waiting room for the judge to come in, I had an overwhelming feeling of peace come over me. I started to pray. I told God that whatever I received in settlement I would share with Ray's foundation. I felt Ray was doing great things for those who had so little.

When the judge awarded my monies, my attorney, also named Raymond, suddenly said, "Your Honor, the monies I should receive from Mrs. Lionetti's case can go to her." I almost fell off the chair. When do you ever hear of an attorney not taking his fees?

As we left the courtroom, I thanked my attorney and asked him why he did that. He responded that I had sent him many clients and this was the least he could do. I then told him how I prayed before the judge came out saying that I would send some of my settlement to the *Ray of Hope Foundation*. I told him how I had felt such peace in the courtroom before anyone came in, and now felt my prayers were answered. *Ask and you shall receive.*

I went home and typed a letter to the *Ray of Hope Foundation* sending a copy to my attorney, along with a check for $500.00. In the letter, I told the story of what had occurred while I prayed in the courtroom and how my attorney, also named Raymond, gave up his fee to me. I once again felt it was no coincidence; God works in mysterious ways.

At the Christmas Rosary I observed some people line up to speak with Ray and ask him for help. I sat and listened to one young girl who said she was a single mother and didn't have money to buy her son any Christmas toys. She just wanted to be able to get him one thing and asked Ray for $50.00. She told how she worked two jobs just to make ends meet. Well, I could certainly identify with her.

Ray called me to him and this lady and said, "We will write you a check for $250.00; your son will have a Christmas." Her shock and tears were wonderful to witness. She couldn't thank Ray enough; he turned to her and said, "Oh no, don't thank me. Thank this lady; Gail is giving you the money." Well I almost fell over. She gave me such a big hug, one that I will never forget; I had to cry. I felt so good that night that I was able to help some little boy have a Christmas. There had been many times while growing up that we had very little money. Later, I had my own children and struggled financially, so I knew what this lady was going through. I walked away feeling like I was on 7th heaven.

When they called the raffle for the picture, Wayne and his wife won it. As they went to the stage to pick it up, I heard from my guides; they told me to tell him not to worry about his job. I had no idea why they said that but I delivered the message as we were leaving the hall. Wayne stopped in his tracks and just looked at me, with a look of shock on his face, and then he went out.

Within a few days I got an email from Wayne. He wanted to know why I said that to him when we were leaving. I replied, "My guides told me to let you know." I asked for his phone number, saying that I would like to talk to him on the phone if it was okay. He sent me his number and I called.

Over the phone, Wayne mentioned that he had asked his mother about the name Robert. It was her brother who passed before Wayne was born. Then he asked me why I mentioned his job. I told him that when he had the picture in his hand I was told to tell him that it would be okay.

Wayne, who was a Jersey City police officer, proceeded to tell me about something that happened on his job. When I asked him where he did patrol, he said Greenville section. Since I was born in the Greenville section, I told him where I grew up. When he told me that was the area where he patrolled, I almost fell off my chair. What were the chances of Wayne working the area where I grew up?

We continued to talk about what I do and how I work with law enforcement agencies around the country. He was very receptive. I felt an instant connection to him and his wife and we became friends.

I spoke with Wayne about growing up in Jersey City and what I went through, saying that my gift started to bloom when I lived there. I told him that I wanted to write a book about my life. We both agreed to try it together. I asked Wayne if there was any way I could go back into the schools. I went to my old neighborhood to see the house where I grew up. He advised me that it was not a great area, but he would take me. I was thrilled.

I wrote a letter to the person who currently lived in the house, explaining that I was going to write my story. I explained that I would be in the area, taking pictures outside of the house. I didn't want her to wonder what I was doing. Wayne got in contact with the Board of Education to see if we could visit the schools I attended, tour the hallways and see the classrooms. Wayne was able to get a date for us to go, so we ventured off to Jersey City.

We first went to the house where my gift began. A gentleman came outside; I introduced myself, asking if they received my letter. He said that his grandmother owned the house and it was okay for me to look around. I had my father's Navy papers with me to show that we did live at that address in 1956. I stood on the sidewalk looking up to the top floor of the two-family house recalling all the memories, most of which were not good.

Wayne surprised me by asking if we could possibly go into the house, which we did on April 9, 2003. I brought the lady a dozen red roses for being so gracious to let us into her home. Minnie was such a nice lady. We talked about my growing up in the house. I noticed that the sun porch where I used to lock myself in was no longer there.

That sun porch was where it all began for me, speaking to my dolls. So many things flashed before me; I wished I could have gone onto that porch again just to remind me of the good times I had hearing the spirit voices.

We had an appointment to go to the schools, so after spending some time with Minnie, I thanked her for allowing me to meet her and come into her home. She said that I could come back anytime. It made me feel good—it took me 44 years to finally feel good in that house.

As we were leaving, I noticed two older ladies climbing steps at the house next door. They were the Gorski's, and I was shocked that they still lived there after 47 years. I introduced myself telling them I used to live in the upstairs part of the house next door back in 1956 to 1959.

They were two sisters who were the only ones alive from that family. Although they didn't quite remember the name Hallam from that time period they remembered the nice good- looking young man who always came in a military uniform. Well, of course, that was my dad. And yes he was a good looking man.

We sat on their steps reminiscing. They took me down memory lane with names that I'd long forgotten. As we talked I could see myself playing in the street as a child. I thanked both sisters for taking the time to walk me back in memories and wished them well. I walked away feeling a little overwhelmed. Going into the home I once grew up in, seeing neighbors who still lived there, and taking the stroll down memory lane brought back so much to me, some good and some sad.

Next, Wayne and I were off to PS-20, the school where I went to from kindergarten to second grade. The memories that I had were not so good. The principal, Mr. Fernando, met us and asked a few questions about what I remembered about PS-20.

I told him I remembered my kindergarten teacher's name, Ms. Bouquet. He was surprised that I still recalled her name and told me that she had passed away three years previously. I was shocked; as a child in school she looked old to me. I realized that maybe she had been only in her early 20's when she taught. I can still see her in my mind so clearly; she was very pretty and so nice to me. I knew she liked Pussy Willows.

My mother's friend owned a florist that was on my way to school. I'd stop in to ask if he could give me some Pussy Willows for my teacher. He wrapped them in green paper and I was on my way to school feeling special. When I gave them to her she was so pleased.

The principal asked if I remembered where my kindergarten class was and I pointed to the left. He responded that I was correct although now it was his office. We went in and my mind flashed upon the classroom, recalling nap times, snack time, and of course play time. He showed me two pictures and I automatically recognized the face of Mrs. Martin, my principal. I always thought she was mean, but then again she had to put up with me because I would not stay in my classroom. I was constantly wandering the hallways and then sent to her office for punishment.

We proceeded upstairs to the auditorium where we used to have plays and assemblies. The thing that was most overwhelming was that as a small child, everything seemed so much bigger. Even in the house I visited, the rooms had seemed much bigger to me until I saw them as an adult. I got up on the stage and looked around the room; it brought so many memories of plays and skits back to my mind.

As we proceeded throughout the school, I saw the room I once sat in; the desks still remained the same. All the woodwork in the school was the same old brown wood. The doors were very heavy with a window at the top that could be opened in a slant position.

Behind the classroom was a coat room where we had to hang our coats or take off our rain boots and leave our lunch boxes until we were ready to eat. There weren't too many coat rooms left in the school. The principal said they were taking them out to make the classrooms bigger. I couldn't believe that I was once again sitting behind a desk in a room I had been in over 47 years ago. What an experience.

As I continued to tour the hallways I popped my head into a classroom where there was a teacher sitting at her desk. I said hello and mentioned to her I was visiting from the past. I told her I was writing a book and recalling all the memories I had of this school.

This teacher asked me what I did now for a living, and I told her that I was a private investigator and also a psychic. She thought it was interesting, and asked where I lived. When I told her, she said she had heard about me, that some of the teachers had talked about me from other schools in Jersey City. I realized that I had read for quite a few teachers from the schools in Jersey City. What a small world.

Wayne and I thanked the principal; I told him it was an experience I would never forget. From there we went to PS-34, a few blocks away. When we arrived at this school we met with its principal Mrs. Merlock. She said she heard about me and was happy to have me visit. She asked a few questions about who I remembered as teachers. I would never forget Miss. Eagen; she had looked like a witch to me (those early childhood thoughts again). She said that Miss Eagen had just retired two years before. *Holy crow,* I thought, *she is still alive.*

I went downstairs to the lunch room. Aside from my surprise at seeing how small it was, it still looked the same. I mentioned to the principal that she should think about hanging class pictures of graduates in the hallways. When someone like me goes back 47 years later, s/he can look and see classmates who attended with them. It could help them remember and reminisce. At the conclusion of the tour, I thanked the principal for allowing me her time and to walk through her school.

What I found out that day was all those who I had the opportunity to speak with were so kind. They took the time to talk to me and allowed me to come into their home or school. They made me feel like I was someone, something I hadn't felt for a long time.

If it weren't for God placing Wayne in my life at that time, these visits would never have occurred. Although I didn't end up writing the book with Wayne, it was the first steps of recalling my childhood memories. I am ever so grateful to him.

◊◊◊

In recognizing that people come into our life for reasons, it is valuable to look deeper into what is being shown to us. As mentioned previously, that person is a *reflection* of ourselves—sometimes we love the reflection, and sometimes we don't. Often, we don't even want to think that the person that we dislike is a reflection of an aspect of ourselves. Nevertheless, it is so.

Gail will frequently recognize similarities between her and new people whom she meets, as she does in the next chapter with some celebrity comedians. I have also asked her to look at how she and her mother are alike...and she has considered that, as well. One aspect that stood out is that her mother, like Gail, was the primary person in raising her children.

◊◊◊

### Celebrity Comedians

In 2003 I met a well-known comedian. He made a few famous movies, including several sequels and this man is incredible. I will call him Matt.

I always wondered how he threw his voice and made the amazing sounds he did in movies. Through his voice, he could make sounds such as nails running across a chalkboard, squeaky shoes walking, a machine gun going off, and a phone ringing. So when I heard he was coming to the Comedy Club, I called to get tickets. I told the manager, whom I knew quite well, that if there was any way I could personally meet this man I would love to. He said he would see what he could do.

The day came and I went to the show, reminding the manager that I'd like to have the opportunity to tell this man what a gift he had. I brought my cousins with me—14 of them—and Wayne and his wife. I thought it would be cool if Wayne got to meet Matt. Of course I didn't have any intention of having all these people meet him, we just all loved him in the movies and this gave us a chance to see him in person. I waited with anticipation and was escorted to the "Green Room."

The manager told Matt that I was a friend of his who wanted to meet him. I am sure all this was planned out before my going there. As we were introduced, I saw a woman in spirit standing behind him with such sadness in her face. I said to myself, *Okay Gail, now what are you going to do?* Also in this room was a man in a suit whom I thought may have been his manager and another man who looked like he was with the Grateful Dead band; he was an older man with long grey hair pulled back in a ponytail. I shook hands with Matt and told him that I truly enjoyed what he did and that it was an honor to meet him personally.

I began communicating with this woman spirit who told me she was the celebrity's wife who passed away. I asked her name and she told me what I thought was Linda; it was spoken to me in such a soft voice that I could hardly hear her. I said to myself, *I have to mention this to Matt because his wife wanted to let him know she was there and doing just fine.* However, I didn't want to say it in front of the other men. His wife yelled to me *Just do it!*

Being put on the spot, I said to Matt, "There is a women standing behind you saying 'Linda.'" He looked at me with shock and responded, "You mean Belinda?" I replied, "Well, she speaks softly; maybe that is it. He told me that was his wife who had passed. I wanted to give more to him, but felt uncomfortable about saying any more in front of the rest of the people in the room.

I looked at the gentleman in the suit and asked if he was Matt's manager. He responded no, saying that he was the limo driver for him. The other man who looked like the Grateful Dead member said, "I am Matt's manager; my name is Brian." Could have fooled me. I asked if it was okay if we could be left alone so Matt could have a conversation with his wife. They all agreed and left the room.

I explained to Matt what I do and asked him if he believed in communicating with the spirit world. He got up from the couch and went into his briefcase and pulled out the book *Talking to Heaven*. Then I really knew it was going to be okay. I proceeded to get her messages through, and both of us felt the emotion. It was a great experience for us.

The call came for him to get downstairs and start his show; he didn't want to leave. It was touching; the showroom was packed with people who came to see him and he didn't want to leave me, speaking with Belinda. I told him that he had to go on stage and he asked if I would stay to see his show. When I told him I was already a paid customer, he laughed and said, "Enjoy the night." He also asked if I would give him my phone number to call; he wanted to speak with me more. I said I would.

The night proved to be very interesting. They always have a lead-in comedian for the headliner of the night. As I and my cousins sat right in the front row—something you never do when you are at a comedy show—we were picked on. This comedian, Roy, noticed I wasn't smiling and asked why I had such a nasty puss on my face. I replied, "You really do not want to mess with me.' He said out loud to the audience "Oh she scares me."

Then he looked at two of my cousins who are brothers and do look very much alike, and asked them if they were the Smith Brothers (from the cough drop box). The Smith brothers wore beards and mustaches and so did my cousins. The funny thing is that they do look like the Smith brothers.

I know comedians need to pick on people in the audience; that is part of the act, but I get insulted easily. I guess I do show a puss on my face in those instances, because I hate being pointed out in an audience. It's the price you pay for sitting in the front row.

Well Roy kept insulting me. He asked why I was holding onto my pocketbook so close, saying "Are you afraid the black people in the audience are going to steal it from you?" Well I got pissed, and I came back with, "I have a 9mm in my pocketbook and will not be afraid to blow your F*)&(& ing head off." That did it for him; the rest of the night he left me alone.

After I watched Matt do his show, I went outside to the dining area. While I was talking to my cousins, Roy, who wouldn't leave me alone, walked in. It was a Kodak moment. His face dropped as he walked towards me, and said "Hey lady, are you a cop or something? Do you really have a gun?" My response to him was "I'll never tell and yes I have a gun." For a moment, he seemed afraid and I had to laugh.

He and I started talking; we talked right through the second show. I asked him why he carried so much anger, which was what I had picked up on him. He said to me "What are you psychic or something?" I loved it. I responded that I was. He told me that he was divorced and, as a comedian traveling all over the country, he seldom saw his child. In addition, he had a painful childhood. I felt that he thought the *world owed him a living*. I shared that I also had a bad childhood and that it had taken me a long time to learn that we need to leave the anger and pain in the past.

As the second show started, Roy said that he was glad to have met me and apologized for picking on me, but also mentioned that I had to lighten up. I said it was a pleasure meeting him. It made me see the sadness, pain and anger comedians carry from life experiences. However, to hear him say that I helped him understand many things in life was good enough for me. I thanked God once again that I was doing what he sent me here to do...to help others.

Matt noticed that I hadn't left. He again asked for my phone number and said he wanted to stay in contact with me. He gave me an autographed video of his show. I insisted that I pay for it, because I do not like accepting things; he said absolutely no, that it was his gift to me for helping him that night.

During the next week I got a call from his manager, Brian, telling me that they would be back in New Jersey the following weekend. He asked if I could come to see Matt again and spend more time with him. I was in awe; this person was a celebrity and wanted to spend time with me—talking with me. He asked if I would like to have a limo pick me up and I said no, that it wasn't necessary. Still, he said they would pay for my food and stay for the weekend.

I got to the Hilton, checked in, read awhile in my room, and then called Brain on his cell phone to let them know I was there. He asked that I meet him at the lounge downstairs because they were doing sound checks. I had a drink of wine because I was nervous. Why?

I don't know. I guess it was my thinking: *Here is this guy from TV who has done many movies, is well known, and he wants me in his presence.* As I believe God puts people in our life for a reason. I went into the showroom, watched them set up for that night's show and then Matt came in. He thanked me for coming and said he was excited to see me.

We had dinner where we could be alone to talk. I was hoping I didn't spill anything on me or drop food out of my mouth...the silly things that come across your mind. What I found out about Matt was that he was just a down-to-earth person.

As he ate his steak, I heard the slurping of soup. Since we had a private table, no one was close to us and it took a moment before I realized that it was Matt making the soup sounds.

During our conversation, the sound of a telephone rang. Matt said, "Your phone is ringing." I replied, "No, it's not my phone because my phone rings with *La Cucaracha*." As it continued to ring, he again advised me that it was my phone and not him. I was certain it was him and I wasn't going to let him embarrass me by answering the phone. The third time he advised me that it really was my phone, I looked at it. A call had come through and a message left. I didn't understand how it rang normally when it was set for *La Cucaracha*. I apologized for being so suspicious of his humor.

We shared about our lives and what we went through as kids growing up, finding out we had a lot in common. As mine, his had not been an easy life. He had a dad who was in the Marines and traveled a lot with family. Being uprooted all the time, he tried to make friends every where he went but it was hard, especially in those days as a young African American child. I told him of my dad being in the Navy and hardly seeing him, because he was always on the ship. Matt had a tough father growing up and I had a tough mother. Each time he had to transfer to different schools it became harder for him, so he would do things to amuse himself and others. I am sure he had teachers going crazy. I would have loved to have been in his classes or *a fly on the wall* when he grew up. I sat again in the audience when he performed and watched in amazement at the talent this man has.

Once again it was shown to me that no matter what we go through in life, we can make something of ourselves. Matt used the tool of comedy as a small child to an adult; it helped him to get by many obstacles that he faced. He did make something of himself and did quite well. He also has to raise the two children his wife left behind, so that makes it more difficult for him.

I walked away that weekend laughing and crying. I said to myself, *These guys who make us laugh carry so much weight on their shoulders. It amazes me how they transform from one person to another, and the smiles they show us, when behind the scenes there is sadness.* I pray for them all, because we as the audience never know what they go through in their life once they walk off a stage.

I met another comedian named Carl. I was called by the manager of the Comedy Club to come see him and see if he was "legit." He advertised himself as the psychic-hypnotist.

When I arrived, I was told the staff had been advised not to tell him who I was and what I did. He was introduced to me and I asked him to do a reading. As I sat watching Carl, I was reading him at the same time. He used a deck of cards which, if I remember correctly, was a regular deck of playing cards. I shuffled them and he laid them out on the table.

He began saying things that did not make sense to me at all. I said to myself, *another person trying to be psychic*; there are so many of that kind out there. Well, as the reading continued I started to ask him some questions. He wasn't able to answer them correctly.

Carl had to wrap up his reading with me because he had to get ready to do a show, but at the last minute he said, "You have to change things around your kids." Well that hit a nerve. I asked him why he said that and he replied that he didn't know.

He began his show as I sat in the audience and watched. The staff asked me what I thought of him after my reading. I gave him credit, saying, "Well he mentioned something about my kids, so he hit on one thing in a 45 minute reading." Perhaps I had been blocking him...what I call "testing." Blocking is shutting down the mind so the psychic can't get energy from you to give a reading. When a person shuts down the mind, he or she is testing the person. When a person is open to me...and not trying to test me...s/he is so much easier to read.

When he started to warm up the audience, Carl said things in a joking way like, "I see someone around you with the letter

M—Mary, Monica, Mommy, yes it is Mommy. You live with your Mommy." Well, that was cute. Then he proceeded to say something along the lines of, "I see money coming to you, lots of money, I see you getting it on Friday." Since Friday is payday for most people, that made me laugh.

When Carl hypnotized people from the audience I watched at how some faked it and others truly were somewhat hypnotized. He didn't do anything to make fools out of people; he was doing it for laughs. After all we were in a comedy club. But there was something I detected in him that I felt that I had to pursue.

When the show was over I went into the bar area and he came over to me. He found out I was psychic, and asked me some questions about whether I thought he has that gift. I told Carl that we all have gifts but it is how we use them that is important. He has the gift of being a comedian. He had made me laugh. We talked about different things and how to open yourself up to receiving more, fine tuning your ability, and meditating.

Once again, I felt that I somehow was to help this man, yet I couldn't put my finger on it. Still, I felt I had to do something for him. I asked him when he was coming back to the club, and he told me it would be two months. I know the comedy club puts them up in a hotel, but I asked him if he would like to come stay at my home and I would teach him how to meditate, to try and to help open him up to receive more.

Two months later he came to my house. We talked and while sitting in my living room I saw a man appear, who told me he was Carl's father, who had crossed over. I asked the spirit, *Do you want me to tell your son you are here?* His father responded, *Of course, I didn't come for nothing.* I thought, *Okay, another comedian.*

I proceeded to tell Carl that his dad was with us in the living room. I asked him who Sal was and he said that was his dad's name. I noticed Carl squirm a little, so I asked him if he was okay to continue speaking with his dad; he said yes. His dad told me that he was hard on his son growing up and that he was so sorry for that and hoped that Carl would forgive him. That brought up emotion for him. I told him it was okay to show emotions, that it was part of cleansing. The conversation went on and by the time we were almost finished we were both grabbing for tissues.

When his dad left us, I asked Carl to just sit in the moment and to release anything he had to release—pain, anger whatever, it was okay. We sat and talked some more; I learned more about the hard life he had with his dad. There was my answer. I knew there was something we had shared together, and I got my answer the day his dad came in. Carl's dad wanted him to know how proud of him he was, and that meant a lot to his son.

While growing up, Carl said his dad never told him that he loved him. As we continued to talk, I told him about my life and the tortures I went through with my mother, but somehow survived.

Carl was appreciative of staying at my house and talking with his father. He gave me an autographed picture of himself, signed with his name and "I see dings."

Once again, I had met a comedian, a man who made people laugh but also carried baggage from his childhood... someone who survived through making people laugh, but walked off the stage with sadness. What I have learned from meeting all these comedians was that they, too, are human and go through things like the rest of us.

## Family Challenges Continue

From my sister's best friend, I learned that Ginger was afraid of dying. She had breast cancer. I shared my near-death experience with my sister and believe that it eased her fear of dying. A year later—to the date—Ginger passed away and I was with her.

The day that I was called to the hospital, the doctor told me that she would not last through the night. At that time, I saw my father appear in spirit and tell me that they were preparing to come to get her at 9:00. I assumed that they both were referring to 9:00 that night. So, I sat by her side as she fell into a coma, held her hand and reminisced with her about things we did together.

I reminded her about the time we had a fist fight in the car, and even though her eyes were half open, I could see the gleam in her eye. I told her how much I loved her and that daddy said he was coming to get her. My mother and brother-in-law sat out in the hospital hallway all night long. It gave me the opportunity to be with her until the end.

It amazed me; every hour on the hour, the nurse would come in and advise me of what organ was breaking down. My sister was bloated with so much fluid that at one point the nurse asked me to help push her to the side so he could put a clean pad underneath her. When I went to push her, my hand sunk in her back, I heard the water swish; she was all yellow. I could not believe what I saw.

Nine o'clock came and went. As I watched the sun rise at 5:30 in the morning, I looked into her eyes, held her hand, and told her that it was time to go. At 8:50 am, my brother-in-law entered the room and said he was going to go to the bank, asking if she would be okay. I told him that I would stay and that she wasn't going anywhere. Soon after he left, I thought I heard her try to say something to me. I hurriedly responded, "I'll be right back; I'll get the nurse." At this time, it was approximately 9:07 am.

When I saw the nurse, I told her that my sister was trying to tell me something and asked her to come to the room. By the look on the nurse's face, I knew she was trying to tell me that she was gone. The nurse did come to her room. She checked her pulse, checked her heart, and said that my sister must have said goodbye to me.

Strange, I thought, when the doctor said that she wouldn't last through the night and my dad said they were preparing to get her at 9:00, she waited for her husband to leave the hospital and the 9:00 became 9:07 am. I soon found out, after my sister's death, that my brother-in-law was having an affair, and she was well aware of it. I felt that she didn't want him to be there when she crossed over; she waited for him to leave.

I felt that my sister never really believed in psychic abilities. Still, she may have had her own gifts that came through dreams. I recalled a phone call from Ginger describing a dream that she had in which a woman came to her job to tell her that she was going to marry Ginger's husband.

Perhaps two months later, a woman did, in fact, go to her job and told her those same, exact, words. Ginger called me immediately, very upset, telling me about the woman coming to her place of employment. I left my own work and drove like *a bat out of hell* to Ginger commenting that if I found this woman, I'd kill her. This happened years before my near-death experience and before I understood how our actions affect others—and ourselves. After my sister's death, my brother-in-law did marry the woman.

My son graduated from high school approximately 10 days after my sister died. It was hard for me to attend what should have been a happy occasion. I missed Ginger not being able to be there with me.

Even though I was an adult with two children, there was still no let up to the problems with my mother. My Uncle Tom, my mother's brother, was 82 years old and very active, living in New York. Somehow in his travels, he fell in the subway and broke both of his hips. He lived alone on the 5th floor of his apartment building and the only people who took care of him were visiting nurses.

One day I called to tell him that I was going to visit and asked what groceries he needed. I went shopping and then drove into New York. This poor man could barely get around in his 2-room apartment, but was so overjoyed that I had come to see him and brought him all the "goodies." We sat and talked for awhile and he was so proud that he was able to walk up and down stairs with a walker. He took me outside his apartment and showed me what he could do on the stairway.

On the first floor, I noticed there was a crack house and a lot of druggies going in and out. I was quite concerned for my elderly uncle. I asked him to be careful to be sure that his doors were always locked. He said that before this accident, in going in and out of the building, they would say, "Hi pops, how are you doing?" He felt they were protecting him.

After a nice visit, the following weekend I got a call from my uncle that my mother had called and yelled at him, demanding to know why he had let me come to see him. She upset him so much that he called me. He didn't understand why she didn't want his niece (me) to visit. He felt that she was harassing him. I told my uncle that I would go to her house to find out what was going on.

Once I got there, my niece came out and said that Gram did not want me on the property. I tried to explain to Dawn that her grandmother was upsetting my Uncle Tom and that I wanted to know why she called and yelled at him. I told Dawn that I did not want to go inside the house, "Just let my mother come to the door and let me speak with her." My niece started poking her fingers into my chest, telling me I had to get off the property. She went to raise her hand at me and a fight ensued. I punched her and eventually went home with blood-drawn scratches all over my face and on my chest.

I called my friend, Dottie, to pick me up and take me to police headquarters. I explained what had happened and wanted to sign a complaint against my niece. While Dottie was on the way, I received a call from another friend who was a state trooper, asking me what street my mother lived on. When I said Buttonwood Place, he said that he heard on the police scanner that a woman threatened to kill her mother and a car was being sent to my home.

Dottie arrived and as I was getting into her car, four police cars arrived at my house. One of the officers asked me to step out of the car. I tried to tell them that I was on my way to police headquarters to sign a complaint. This officer knew our family. He advised me, once again, to step out of the car and said he had to place me under arrest. While putting on handcuffs, he was rough-housing me, proceeding to hit my head as I got into the police car. I asked why he was being so rough with me, "What did I do?" His response was, "You know what it is like to treat an inmate." I responded, "I don't treat inmates like this."

As this was going on, my daughter was standing in the doorway, thoroughly confused. My friend, Dottie was yelling, "Don't treat her like that." They threatened Dottie to keep quiet or she would be charged with obstruction of justice. Off I went in the police car. As I sat in the back of the car, I spoke to my father in spirit, saying, *Dad, do you believe what she has done to me again?*

I asked the officer why I was being arrested. I was read my Miranda rights and told that I had threatened to kill my mother. At police headquarters I was taken in the back and handcuffed to a bench. Again, I asked another officer why I was being held. He replied, "Your mother called and said that you went to her house and threatened to kill her." "I didn't even see my mother; I spoke to my niece," I responded.

At no time was I fingerprinted or photographed. I was asked if there was anything they could get me. I asked for water and to see my daughter, who was waiting in the lobby. Although they said okay, I neither got the water nor saw my daughter.

The officer returned and stated that I was being released on my own recognizance and I would be receiving papers to appear in county court. I walked out of there knowing that I had been falsely arrested. Knowing the laws, if I had truly threatened to kill my mother, I would have had to post bail. Also, they hadn't fingerprinted or photographed me.

When I appeared at county court, I asked a friend to observe my mother as she walked into the court room. When my case was called, my brother led my mother by her arm up to the bench and seated her, as if she needed help. (My friend later told me that she had walked in with no assistance or problems).

The judge questioned my mother as to what happened. It seemed that one could hear a pin drop in the court room. She proceeded to tell him that I came over and threatened to kill her. There was a gasp from the audience.

The judge asked me for my statement. I explained that I had never gotten along with my mother throughout my life. The last time that I had seen her was a year previously when my sister passed away. I explained the phone call that I received from my uncle and that I promised him that I'd go talk to her. I told the judge what happened between me and my niece when I got to the house. At no time did I ever threaten to kill my mother, nor did I even see her that day.

After both testimonies, the judge found me not guilty and told me that he would take the restraining order off me. I replied, "To make my mother feel better, maybe you should leave it on." However, I also questioned that if I drove on her street, I wanted to know the distance that I needed to be from her house. I visited friends who lived on the same street, and didn't want her calling the police station when I went to see them. He advised me, "50 feet from the curb," and I agreed.

Unknown to me at the time, this incident would cause actions by my mother that would continue to hurt me.

Two weeks after my father passed away, I found my mother and my daughter overcome by carbon monoxide at my mother's house. I saved them both by arriving at the time that I did, giving my mother 5 more years to her life. The fright of almost losing my daughter was overwhelming since I had just buried my father. My children were regularly supportive to their grandmother; Vinny visited daily and Kim stayed overnight.

A year after the above court case, my mother passed away and I called for the will. What I noticed was that it was dated 3 days after the court case. She left a statement in her will that I was to get nothing. Although I hadn't expected anything, what was most disturbing is that she also left my children out of her will. The fact that my brother got everything and my children received nothing bothers me to this day.

In June 1990, I was still grieving over the death of my sister when my daughter graduated. While taking photos of her preparing for graduation, she yelled at me; she didn't want me to take pictures while she was doing her hair and getting ready. Her outburst, however, made me feel that my mother was yelling at me all over again. There were so many things that I saw in my daughter that reminded me of my mother; it felt like such a painful reoccurrence in my life.

After the event, I went back home, feeling overburdened with my sister's death, my best friend's son who had been killed in a car accident 6 months prior and would have been graduating at the same time, and flashbacks of my relationship with my mother now being played out with my daughter.

Because I hadn't been sleeping, I took 3 or 4 sleeping pills and laid down on the couch to rest. The telephone rang with a friend inquiring about how graduation went. She asked if I was okay because I sounded groggy. I told her that I had taken some sleeping pills to try to get some rest. The next thing I knew, three men were standing over me and an ambulance was outside. My front door was unlocked and they had been called by my friend, who had confused my grogginess with an attempt to take my life. It had never been my intention to commit suicide—I was just trying to get some sleep.

The next thing I knew, I woke up in the emergency room with my son at my side and a woman asking questions. I tried to explain to her that I was sad because of the loss of my sister, that today my daughter was graduating, and that my best friend's son should have been graduating, but had been killed in a car accident, and that I hadn't gotten much sleep for weeks. I explained that I had taken sleeping pills and the next thing I knew a doctor came in and said they were going to pump my stomach.

I questioned why they were going to do that because I hadn't taken an overdose of pills. Still, it was based on the reports so they had to pump my stomach. As they were putting tubes down my nose, it felt as if they were forcing it and I saw blood shooting out all over. I became frightened and angry; they were hurting me. I started fighting the doctor to push him away. I remember kicking him between the legs and at that time they called hospital security.

Security personnel came and restrained my arms and legs. I began to cry, asking why they were doing it to me. The doctor asked if I would take Epicat, in order to make myself vomit. I agreed. After my vomiting, the doctor found no evidence of an overdose of pills. A woman from social services came to ask more questions. I repeated my story and she asked if I wanted to talk to somebody and I said yes, thinking that I'd be talking to a nurse.

I was asked to sign a sheet for my personal belongings. I wanted to read the sheet, but the woman assured me that it was just for my personal belongings. I didn't realize that I was admitting myself to the hospital.

I was wheeled to the east wing, which was the psychiatric ward. Once there, another doctor came to talk to me. He didn't seem interested in what I had to say, just read the reports, and said that he could not release me and that I had to stay. I became very upset because, once I realized where I was, I felt I had no business being there.

I refused to stay in one of the rooms that I would have had to share with someone else. When a nurse talked to me, I explained everything that had occurred that day. She understood the pain and grief that I was carrying and said that I really did not belong there. She said she would contact another doctor to help get me out.

The next day the second doctor arrived and I explained all that had occurred the previous day. I even had him laughing, telling him that I had gone through a 5-hour psychological test for a former job and they had not found me "crazy," although I had some suspicions about the doctor. This physician agreed that I didn't belong there. He stated that if I would take one pill to get some sleep, he would discharge me the next day.

During the rest of my hours there, I tried to help others; even the nurses were impressed. The movie "One Flew over the Cookoo's Nest" taught me that if you're not crazy going into such a place, you will be before you get out.

Even in the grief of her son's death, Ann Marie and her mom came to see me in the hospital. We all ended up laughing together as I told them some of the stories of what went on in the hospital...such as one man playing ping pong with someone who wasn't there. My comment, "Even I can't see this person," caused us all to chuckle.

## Hope for Repairing the Family

While vacationing in Florida with my friend Pat, we sat around having appetizers at her sister's house. It was Thanksgiving and a neighbor, Vinny, came over to wish a Happy Thanksgiving. As we were introduced, I noticed a man in spirit standing next to him. I asked the spirit who he was and he told me he was Vinny's dad. This spirit was smiling, expressing how proud he was of his son. So I had to figure out how I was going to approach this and give the message.

Pat mentioned to Vinny that I am a Private Investigator in New Jersey and he proceeded to tell me that he was a former police officer. I asked Vinny where he was originally from and he said Babylon, NY. I remembered that I had a cousin who lived in Babylon. My guides chimed in and said, *Go ahead, ask him.* I asked him if he knew a man named Mike Flannery. He replied "Yes, he was my neighbor who lived across the street." I almost fell off the chair (yes, this is an expression and feeling that I often have). He mentioned that my cousin helped him with his son, who had seizures. What were the odds? That is why I do not believe in coincidences.

Now I really had to be careful since most police do not believe in psychic perception. So I told him how I worked with the National Center of Missing and Exploited Children to help them find missing kids, most of whom have been abducted and killed. I explained that I am on a database throughout the United States and abroad working with law enforcement agencies. He found it to be interesting, so I figured this was my opening.

I asked if his dad had passed away, and he said yes. I told him he was standing next to him. Well of course shock came over his face. I had to make sure I didn't embarrass him with the others in the room, so I gave him some messages. I saw he was getting overwhelmed and emotional with it. I told him that before we left the next day, I would meet with him so he could speak with his dad privately.

Pat decided she wanted to drive all the way back that night. I felt bad because I had promised Vinny I would connect him with his dad. I was able to get his phone number and e-mail address, so I figured, *What the heck let me email him.*

As I was e-mailing Vinny, his dad came in and gave me some names. I shared them with Vinny in the e-mail. Then I got the overwhelming smell of a cigar, so I asked Vinny who smoked cigars... and who was Nick? Vinny's dad also mentioned the name Rob, and I saw a man standing in front of me who was holding his heart, which usually means a heart attack or heart problems.

Vinny responded, saying that his grandfather used to smoke cigars; his mom had told him this. The man I saw holding his heart was his grandfather; he died of a heart attack. The name Nick was his dad's friend, and Vinny's niece was dating a guy named Rob. There was so much information coming through, I decided to call Vinny instead of using e-mail. He was amazed by all of this. I apologized for not being there in person.

As we talked, his dad came again. I told him that his dad could hear what we were saying and if there was anything he wanted to say or ask he could do so. Before Vinny could say anything, his dad told me he saved his son from an accident in a blue vehicle. I mentioned this and his emotions surfaced. He said that he always knew it was his father who saved him.

His dad mentioned the name Joe, and Vinny said that was the name of his grandfather. Vinny, (Vinny's dad), mentioned he was happy that his wife went on with her life. He gave me the name "Lou" who was Vinny's step dad. The spirit said he would be leaving his daughter (Vinny's sister) dimes. Vinny e-mailed me at a later time and said she was receiving dimes all over the place.

When I was able to see Vinny again, I told him about my background as a child and also of my cousin, Mike, (Vinney's former neighbor), what Mike grew up with, and that he too had survived a bad childhood. My mother had kept Mike out of my life for some reason; she was good at doing that. I told Vinny that I am a true believer that God puts people in our life for many reasons, and that I felt in time, whether it be this year, next, or 3 years down the road, somehow he would be my connection to my speaking with Mike again. I emphasized that I was not pressuring him to call my cousin, but somehow he would be the one to get us back in touch.

When Vinny was leaving, he told me was going to call my cousin; he wanted Mike to know what a beautiful person I was, how we met and how I helped him. He hoped that would bring us back together. I told him of the lies my mother told and the proof I have in writing. As far as Mike knows, his Aunt Mary (my mother) was so nice; of course, he didn't live with her. It was not a coincidence that God placed Vinny in my path.

◊◊◊

Some people who come into our lives help us along the way. They may a brief one-time assistance, or be a constant help, offering physical, mental, or emotional support. Others push us, stretch us, and force us to grow. Whether they do this in a loving or what we perceive to be a hurtful or negative manner, it can serve our soul's lessons and expansion.

# Little Children Shall Lead Us

Some very special souls are being born into these times. Perhaps due to more birth mothers having the opportunity to choose natural childbirth over drugs – or the evolutionary shift that is occurring, it appears that infants coming into the world seem to be more alert and able to think independently than those born during the 1940s or 50s.

Today's young children seem to know, and speak, their minds with more certainty and forcefulness. We might view this as the vastly different child rearing (from the "children should be seen and not heard" attitude) of the past to parents who encourage, or respond to their child's expression with more acceptance. Perhaps the spirits of these children bring a wisdom that is needed in these times. Whatever the reasons, many children today are immediately viewed as very special by the adults around them.

It is not unusual for a child today to speak openly about his or her past life – or seeing a spirit. They take it for granted, and it is natural to them.

One of my colleagues, Carol Bowman, has written a book about children who remember their past lives.[3] In her research she discovered that there are four signs that a child is speaking of an actual past life memory, instead of fantasy:

- Matter-of-fact tone
- Consistency over time
- Knowledge beyond experience
- Corresponding behavior and traits

Occasionally, Gail has met some very special children through parents who have gone to her for readings. She speaks about a few of them.

◊◊◊

---

[3] Bowman, Carol, *Children's Past Lives: How Past Life Memories Affect Your Child.* . Bantam Books, January 1998. [Used with permission].

When parents bring photos of their children, I notice that some are very gifted. I start to describe what the child is going through to get confirmation from the parent; i.e., doesn't sleep well, wakes up tired, having a tendency to be in their own little world, or just wanting to be alone in a room playing by himself/herself. The parents agree that I've described what is happening.

I explain that they are gifted children who have been chosen and placed here to help bring spirituality into this world. It is their children who will change the world. Some are in awe and some are afraid. I can see it in the children's eyes. Some are aggressive – I often have a visual image of a steamroller and these children will not allow anything to get in their way. They are here to do what they were sent to do and want to be known. These children are often mis-diagnosed with ADD or ADHD.

Some other children are passive; their calming work is behind the scenes. There was one child named Jonathon who at the age of two was brought to me by his parents. I thought he was so cute; he came in wearing cowboy boots and a hat. Actually, the parents came for individual readings and when Jonathon walked into my house, he stopped and starred up at my ceiling. I watched his eyes roam from one side of the room to the other. Jonathon said to me, "Do you know that you have beautiful angels here?"

I knew that he was seeing angels; however I tried to trip him up by commenting, "Yes, you mean the angels (statues) in my living room?" He quickly responded, "No, they are up there," pointing to the ceiling. He said that he liked what he felt, saying that my room was "very calming." This floored me—*a little two year old! Where is he getting these things from?*

Nearly two years later, Jonathon's mother called and said that he wanted to see the "lady who has all the angels in her home." She also said that he could not stop talking about me. While on the phone, his mother told me that Jonathon's Poppy (grandfather who was still alive) came to him [out-of- body or astral travel] and said he was getting ready to go to be with Jesus and the angels. The mother told me that a week later, her father, Poppy, died of a massive heart attack. I got chills over my body and wondered *He is only four years old; what kind of a gift does this child have!*

Jonathon's mother said that he tells them things that will happen days and weeks before they occur. In addition, he easily communicates with Jesus. The parents had to take him out of pre-school because he told the other kids about his Poppy being in heaven with Jesus. One boy said, "There is no heaven," and Jonathon hit him in the nose. The parents decided to take Jonathon out of pre-school. It was easier than trying to explain his psychic abilities.

I've had children come to speak to me about their gifts. Looking into their eyes, I could see they were "old souls." The term "old soul" means that they have lived many lifetimes and have gained wisdom.

A boy named Timmy, age 11, came to see me. When I looked into his eyes, I saw that he had been an old sea captain in one of his past lives. I asked if he liked to be around water...or if he liked boats. He started to describe an old wooden ship; he said the name of the ship is in black letters. He went on, "I can see dark black, carved in—it must have been painted over—and the letter C." He seemed to get excited when he began to recall the memory.

Jorge, age 13 said to his mother, "I need to talk to somebody who can understand me. This is something far beyond your comprehension. And, I do not want to go to a doctor and be placed on pills because they think I'm crazy."

When Jorge had quiet time, such as reading a book, he heard spirit voices. He began putting the fan on so he wouldn't hear them.

He said he heard a voice awhile back. "I was lying on my bed Sunday night. It sounded female, around the age of 19 or 20, a young woman. I think it was a call for help. Someone was chasing her. I couldn't really understand, though. This was the first time that I heard a voice and actually knew what was going on. I told her she should come back another time because I had no idea what I was doing...very inexperienced in this." Jorge started hearing voices at the age of 5.

I asked if he thought it was a good or a bad spirit. I explained that if it was a bad one that he would have a very uneasy feeling...and that he was just to use a stern voice and tell it to leave.

# Communicating with Guides and Spirits

Through meditation, psychic readings, or spontaneous paranormal contact, some people discover energies or spirits which seem to be "guides" to them. A guide may come in the form of a loved one who has passed over or a spiritual teacher who comes in the form of anything from a Native American Indian to a monk, gypsy, or court jester...and everything in between. A guide may also appear as an animal or one's Higher Self.

Generally, it is accepted that a guide has had earth incarnations and evolved to a stage of readiness to serve in such a capacity. Some of us may have served as guides when we were in spirit. On the other hand, a spirit, such as a deceased loved one, may be around a person yet not be a guide. It seems that an angel has not had an earth incarnation.

A guide may stay with a person throughout his/her lifetime; another may come in to serve or help a person through a specific purpose or time period. Some guides help with more *earth plane issues*, such as helping to find something that is lost...or helping with a task. Others have little interest in the earth plane; they are only interested in the evolution of the soul. Thus, guides can operate from very different vibratory levels. We can benefit from connecting to any of these levels for assistance in our lives.

Whether a guide is an external energy or one that is a projection of the mind can be debated; however, the guide will often give information that the person does not consciously know.

A guide will not interfere in a person's life—free will to make positive choices or poor choices in one's life remains with each of us and is one of God's greatest gifts. Still, guides or deceased loved ones will sometimes help us, as indicated in a previous chapter by Vinny, who sensed his father's spirit assisting him through an automobile accident.

Over the years, I have studied and researched numerous people during psychic readings, trance medium- ship, and remote viewing. Information that comes through in a psychic reading may come from the psychic picking up on the subject's probable future or from their energy field. In other words, a psychic reading may bring information about a potential future...or consist of feedback of one's own desires carried in their thoughts, emotions, and energy field.

Information can also come to the psychic through a guide or a spirit, which could be connected to either the reader or the subject. Depending upon how clear the channel is *on that day*—and how open or closed the subject is—the messages given may be accurate or inaccurate.

Gail has a strong connection to her guides. Whether during the writing of this book, driving her car, at home, giving a psychic reading, or doing one of her shows, she stays in constant communication with these beings. She has a history with them and trusts them implicitly.

In this chapter, we get a glimpse into how natural it is for Gail to connect with spirits. One challenging part is often figuring out how to deliver messages from a spirit to the unsuspecting person (often stranger) standing next to her. Again and again, she receives confirmation related to the message coming through.

◊◊◊

## Discovering My Guides

I had been taught that we all have guides, and I was curious about how to connect and learn more about them. I found through meditating they sometimes show themselves to you.

As I started meditating I called upon my highest spiritual guide to come in. I connected with an Indian chief. He was very tall, dressed all in white, and had a headdress from head to toe with all white feathers. His face appeared to be a copper-tone color, leathered, yet when I touched his face, it felt so soft. I acknowledged him and asked his name. When I didn't get a response, I named him *Chief White Feather.*

In the meditation, he took me to a beautiful, peaceful and calm mountain top that could have been over the Grand Canyon. Chief White Feather put his right hand at his left shoulder and slowly brought it out directly in front of him 180 degrees. In that span, I saw so many visions of what was to come, some good and some frightening. When he saw that I was getting scared, he said, "Little one, I am here to guide and protect you."

Months later, during a different meditation I connected with another guide. An eagle appeared, flying above me and showed me that he would take me to many heights. He, too, seemed to lift me up as if I were gliding with him looking down. I saw some of the devastation that is to come. I asked his name, and all I got was *Eagle*. I recall his saying that the earth is being changed and somehow I was to help. I asked what I was to do and was told that it would be shown to me at another time.

Soon after that, I connected with another guide who called himself, *Grey Wolf*. He is, in fact, a grey wolf. He is with me at all times, not only during readings but also as I'm traveling, talking on the telephone, and at home. Especially when I forget things, he is the first one to remind me. Since he is always with me, he is the easiest one to communicate with and has a really good sense of humor. Grey Wolf has forewarned me on different occasions, and when I didn't listen, I paid the consequences.

For example, a friend called who owned a business and asked me for a favor. She had a customer who was constantly giving her bad checks. I wondered why she kept accepting them. She asked if I would go to the house of this person and kind of *strong-arm* them into paying her. Immediately I heard Grey Wolf say, *No,* very sternly.

However, I felt bad for her because she was in dire straights and on the verge of losing her business. I told her that I would help. Since I used to do collections, I figured it was *a piece of cake.* A couple of days later, she called to remind me, asking if I'd still help her. I said yes. Grey Wolf immediately said, *Do not leave the house.* But I did.

I went to the post office first to get my mail. I never open my mail in the car; I always take it home...but on this day I took the time to open my mail. Then I started off to meet her.

As I was driving down the street, I noticed a red vehicle approaching a stop sign, but it wasn't stopping. I immediately blew the horn and started to go into the oncoming lanes to get away from the woman driver. She kept coming through the stop sign, directly at me and hit my car broadside.

I knew right then and there that Grey Wolf was still trying to stop me. He was blocking me from going to where I wasn't supposed to be. On my cell phone, I immediately called my friend and left a message saying that I was just in an accident and wouldn't be there.

The next day I found out that she went by herself and the person pulled a gun on her. That's why Grey Wolf told me *No,* and to not leave the house. He knew my *bully nature* would have come out. I would have strong-armed this person and possibly been shot.

I apologized to Grey Wolf for not listening to him and thanked him for the accident. I promised that I would always listen to him. And, from that time on, I have listened and followed his guidance to the letter.

Several years later, my friend, Angel, was in town from Florida with a Christmas present for me. Unfortunately, I wasn't able to see her at that time. Seven months later, her sister-in-law dropped the gift off, still wrapped in Christmas paper. I thought of *Christmas in July.* I was receiving a Reiki attunement; a balancing of energy. I took the gift and put it in the kitchen to open later.

During the energy balancing, I called upon my guides. Although I didn't feel them around me, I heard drumming. I opened my eyes to peak and see where the sound was coming from. I saw at my feet, to my left, was an Indian warrior drumming. To my right was an Indian holding a staff with an arrowhead attached at the top. I welcomed them, listened to the drumming, and felt an abundance of energy coming towards me.

In my third eye (a channel of psychic vision), I saw an image of a buffalo so big, right in front of me. I opened my eyes to peak and saw this buffalo, as plain as day, right in my face. Imagine having a huge buffalo in your living room. I didn't hear a name come from him, so I called him *Buffalo Bill,* remembering that from childhood.

After the attunement was completed, I opened my Christmas present. I was shocked at what I held in my hands. A totem of an eagle, an Indian face, a wolf, and at the bottom was a buffalo. I had just connected with the buffalo and here it was on this totem. I guess I wasn't supposed to have it seven months previously, until I made connection with the buffalo.

However, for months, I didn't have any communication from the buffalo until one day when I was brushing my teeth. I looked into the mirror and saw the buffalo standing behind me. I saw the look on his face and through mental telepathy perceived that he didn't like his name. I heard him say, *Lakota*. I acknowledged it and looked up the name Lakota on a Native American site and learned that it means, "friend."

It was only while Janet and I were writing this book that I learned more about the name Buffalo Bill. I had thought he was a fictional cowboy. Janet's husband said that he was actually William Cody, and given the name *Buffalo Bill* because he slaughtered so many buffalos. It prompted us to go on internet; we both were shocked. We learned that Buffalo Bill was known as the champion buffalo killer of the Great Plains. According to one site, he killed 4,280 buffalo in 17 months alone.

Now I realize why the buffalo guide didn't appear or communicate with me after I called him *Buffalo Bill*. Apparently I had more to learn. Being such an animal lover, I now understand the impact that name could have on this spirit.

Once again during a meditation, I felt a breeze above my head. In times such as this, I open my eyes to be sure that I'm not imagining things. A beautiful white Eagle was flying above my head and I had such peace. In this instance, the guide gave me its name, *White Eagle*. I acknowledged him and continued to meditate as he hovered over me.

Over the years, I've learned that the guides have been assigned to me for different purposes. Chief White Feather seems to appear when I feel fear; he assures me that he will protect me. Eagle lets me know when something isn't right, so I become more alert to my surroundings. When I'm sad, White Eagle brings peace.

I have to say, Grey Wolf is the biggest communicator and has a sense of humor to go along with it. He keeps my life interesting. Sometimes he interferes with my conversations (in a good way) and always guides me when I'm doing readings. If there is something that's not coming in clearly, he clarifies it for me. Grey Wolf is also my memory enhancer; he constantly reminds me of things I'm forgetting. For example, even when I'm packing for a trip, he *barks out*, things that I may forget to take. If it weren't for him, I don't know where I'd be.

In addition to the guides that work most closely with me, I have others. Two black crows that I call, *Heckle and Jeckle* assist my travels. One day, as I took a shuttle bus to Newark airport and was stuck in traffic, I looked out the window. On the shoulder I saw the two crows walking northbound. They were telling me that once I got to the airport and took off, I'd connect with two hawks to continue my journey. In New Jersey, Heckle and Jeckle help me to get to where I need to be...then the hawks greet me as I leave New Jersey and travel with me, forewarning any problems that may arise. My guides communicate with me in a variety of ways.

We each have one or sometimes several animal guides around us. Some are permanent guides and others are transitory in nature. These animal guides connect us to the wisdom of Mother Earth. The best way to connect with these guides is to notice which animals you have an affinity towards. Are you attracted to eagles, bears, cats, dogs, dolphins, or others? The ones a person feels most drawn to may be his/her guides.

Since love is the most powerful force in the universe, the people we love and who love us are near us, whether emotionally, in physical body or the other side. These helpers or guides are watching over us, channeling love and support as we go about our daily lives. Their communication to us is to give assurance that life is eternal and that we are never alone. It is best to accept their support, but also to release them to go about their own growth on the other side. If we become too attached to someone who has crossed over we might delay their progress and growth, as well as ours.

Light beings are highly advanced souls who may appear as a flash of light, column of light, or ball of light. They are physically manifesting around us to get our attention. They have a message for us and once that message has been received will move on to their next mission. They are the communicators of the universe. Acknowledge their presence and ask for the message to be given in a way that can be understood.

The first step to connecting with any of these spirit guides is an openness and willingness. They are always there and waiting to connect. We need to find a time to allow the mind to be quiet and meditate. It is best to pick a regular time to do this and be consistent. I meditate in the morning and afternoon.

In the beginning, until comfortable with the process, visualize being enclosed in a bubble of white light. Ask for those that are the highest spiritual beings to be with you and your purpose.

## Turtle Guides: Helping a Friend Discover Her Guides

I was on vacation in Florida in 2004, spending two weeks to rest up from a rough year. While I was with my friend Pat, I tried to teach her how to connect with her guides. I explained to her about my guides who travel with me. As I mentioned earlier, I have two hawks and two black crows who I call Heckle and Jeckle from the cartoon I used to watch as a child.

After sunning ourselves, and my skin looking like a lobster, Pat and I decided to leave the beach. I noticed my two hawks gliding above us with such a beautiful wing span. At that moment I felt that I was gliding up with them and I had an out-of-body experience. I felt so peaceful, flying above with not a care in the world for those few moments. Looking below, I watched Pat as she was packing up so we could go to her home. Unfortunately I had to come back to reality.

I explained to Pat, "They are trying to warn me that something is going to happen, but we will be okay." As we walked from the beach, we crossed the street to her dad's house where we left her car. I noticed something half in the road and half in the grass. It was a huge black and orange snake. I yelled out to watch where she was walking and Pat headed right for it because she didn't know where it was. We are both terribly afraid of snakes. Still, we continued down the street without a care.

Once we started thinking about what took place, however, we agreed that it had been a close call. The surprising thing is that we didn't even run away from the snake. It was strange that we didn't automatically throw a beach chair or something at it. Pat reminded me that my guides had warned us and also said we would be okay. Perhaps this assisted in showing Pat more about how our guides help us.

On Thanksgiving Day, we headed out to Boca Raton to Pat's sister's house. As we were driving I noticed something ahead in the road that appeared to be a garbage bag. A car passed us on a 2 lane road and drove over it, but Pat hit it. We heard such noise under the carriage of the car. I didn't want to know what it was but Pat said it was a turtle. I was so upset because I am such an animal lover; I hate to see animals hurt.

Right away I communicated with the turtle and it answered me saying that his shell was cracked but he would be okay. Yes, the turtle was speaking to me. I advised Pat that the turtle was okay and not to worry. I then thought to myself, *Why is it that the guy in front of us didn't hit the turtle; possibly he had a higher under carriage.*

There was such silence in the car so I figured I'd joke, "I wonder if Lois is serving turtle soup." Pat moaned "Oh no! Don't say that!" I continued, "Geez I wonder if she has those candies called Turtles." They are a caramel chocolate covered candy.

We laughed, but I still pondered, *Why did Pat wind up hitting that turtle?* My mind never shuts down. I felt perhaps this had to happen while I was with her to connect her to her guide, which I thought could be the turtle.

We arrived at her sister, Lois' house and I continued harassing, "Pat is a murderer; she hit a turtle on the way here." Yes I didn't give up on this, but we all laughed.

I had visited Pat's home throughout the years. I was out by her pool talking on my cell phone when something caught my eye. I looked at the patio bar and saw a turtle candle holder. I said to myself, *I never noticed that before as being a turtle.* Then I looked around and noticed she had turtle planters by the pool, in fact there were four of them. I started to laugh at another turtle that I saw. It was made of fabric on the top of a stake and when the wind blew his little legs moved in the wind.

I asked Pat, "How many years have I been coming here and you had these planters out by the pool?" I continued, "Look Pat, what are they? She looked around with amazement and said, "Oh my God—turtles."

I responded, "Yes, for sure." I told her she had to hit that turtle to find out that was one of her guides, and I had to be in Florida to connect it for her. If I hadn't been there and she had hit the turtle she would not have given it any more thought other than feeling bad about it.

We went to the beach once again and a lady who passed us had a turtle on her shirt. I pointed it out to Pat; she laughed. Coincidence? No. We went out to an Italian restaurant that night, and guess what— on the menu was Turtle Cheesecake. Why in God's name would a restaurant call cheesecake Turtle Cheesecake.

As we left the restaurant, we were on a road we had traveled many times, A1A a major highway along the Florida coast. Pat lived off A1A. We passed a community called Turtle Bay. We looked at each other; she was getting it. Turtles were all around her. I connected her to her guide, told her to acknowledge it and give it a name. The turtle was here to help her.

## Ghost Tour

Before my vacation started, Pat and I had talked about going on a Ghost Tour in St. Augustine, Florida. The town dates back to the Nation's oldest city founded in 1565. There was sure to be a lot of spirits walking around. We arrived at the hotel, checked in and decided to walk into town and take in the sights. Pat and I signed up for the tour and had to return at 9:00 pm. When we went back to the hotel to freshen up, we chose a restaurant to get something to eat.

As we got into her car, I noticed my window was half way down. I hadn't opened it during the ride so I thought it was odd. I mentioned it to Pat and said, "Okay, here we go; spirits are playing with us." I warned Pat, "You wanted to experience spirits, so be ready." We got to the restaurant, and I commented, "Let's be sure the windows are up." They shouldn't have been down because it was hot and we drove with the air conditioner on. So we both walked around the car and all windows were closed.

When we came out we looked at the front windows not paying attention to the back ones and while we were driving I heard a noise. I looked in the back; the window was open a little more than a quarter of the way down. With this as a beginning, it made me wonder what we were going to experience on the Ghost Walk.

As we sat waiting for the other participants, two guys came and sat at a picnic table in front of us. I noticed a spirit come in and say, "Paul." I told Pat, what just happened and said, "I don't know who Paul is, but he belongs to one of these guys." She asked me if I was going to say anything to them. Of course said no, I still have a thing about people thinking I'm "nuts."

We began the tour, and went to a Fort called Castillo de San Marcos. Once I stepped on the grounds, the hair stood up all over my body and I felt there had been lot of torture in that place. I suggested to Pat to hold her hands out somewhat with her palms up and open while on the tour. That would help her to feel the energy of spirits.

After the tour guide introduced himself and told of the history of the fort, we started walking. I went off by myself. Well...I was being pulled in a direction so I went with it. I didn't like what I felt; there was something breathing on my neck and I said to whatever it was, "Leave me alone." When I said that, I could feel more about it. It was big and I didn't like the feeling at all. I spoke once again, with more sternness in my voice, "Leave me alone."

When communicating with spirits, sometimes I have to let them know who is boss, so to say. Harry, the tour guide, heard me and asked what I was getting. I told him that I had a spirit with me that I didn't like.

Harry had his digital camera and snapped a shot of me standing there. When I looked into his camera to view the image, there was an orb sitting on top of my head. It was huge.

**Gail on Ghost Tour**

When I noticed the guy standing next to me, I went ahead and asked him if he knew a Paul,. He said, "Yes that was my uncle, but he died." I told him that Paul was with him on the tour. I didn't know how he was going to take it.

We continued walking, and when we reached a wall, I felt there had been torture and had difficulty breathing. I held my chest and needed to get away from that area. Harry saw I was in distress and asked if I was okay. I replied, "Something very bad happened here, like a lot of killings." He told me we were standing at a firing wall, where they shot soldiers. My God it was horrible.

As I walked away, I saw a spirit at the top of the fort walking back and forth with a musket in his hand, as if he were standing watch. I pointed this out and two guys also saw him. That was where the orb showed up again. We left the Fort and crossed the street to go to a cemetery.

As we went through two big pillars by the walking mall, Harry gave some background to a story. He told of a girl (spirit) who was often seen in between these pillars very late at night. Police, while patrolling the area, noticed this little girl standing by the pillars. They got out of the police car and walked towards her to ask where her parents were. All of a sudden, the girl just disappeared in front of them.

As Pat and I walked through the pillar, I heard a girl scream in my ear, "Molly." It hurt my eardrum; it was so loud. I turned to Pat and told her what had just happened. At that moment, someone else on the tour felt a presence. I turned around and asked "Does anyone know a girl named Molly?" The guy who's uncle was Paul, had a shocked expression on his face and said "That was my daughter who died." Pat said I was spooking her out.

**Ghost Cemetery (Night)**

I told the man that Molly said it was an accident. She yelled that she was okay. He laughed at the yelling and explained that Molly often yelled because she had Down syndrome. He believed that her death had been an accident. A doctor was treating her; however something else caused her death. I didn't go into it with him, but I did tell him to speak with her. I explained that she is very much around him, and she no longer has Down syndrome; she is whole again. He thanked me.

I commented to Pat that I felt as if I were taking the attention away from the tour but also wanted to get the message through. I apologized to Harry, but he said he was finding this all very interesting. Yes, he figured out I was psychic. He also said he never had this much action on the tour before. I said to myself, *Imagine if I were giving this tour every night, the spirits would never leave me alone, pushing to get messages through to people.*

We then went to a cemetery that had some haunts going on, but then, what cemetery doesn't? We walked around the outside of the graves; I kept getting all kinds of energies, but didn't want to deal with it. We came to a headstone. It was so old that I couldn't even read the name on it, but it showed a face.

**Ghost Cemetery (Day)**

What I am totally shocked about, is that when I took the picture in the daylight I could not see a face. Yet, when the photo was developed, I could clearly see the face. We learned that the face on the tombstone shows up only at night. It belongs to a young woman whose name was Helen Porter Baldwin, affectionately known as Nellie, who died at the age of 16 of typhoid fever in 1859.

She was supposedly the most beautiful young woman in town at the time, and her loss was greatly mourned, especially by her sweetheart, a young fellow named Andrew Anderson. He was away at Princeton at the time of her death. Her funeral was held at dawn, and other young ladies were the pall-bearers.

We approached a parking lot, and as we got closer, I spontaneously grabbed my neck. I felt my neck get slashed, at the front, from left to right; the pain was excruciating. I crisscrossed my arms across my heart to block any negative energy around me. With my left hand, I held my neck; I felt as if there was liquid running over my hand. It felt so real that I was afraid to let go of my neck in fear I would bleed to death.

Harry noticed what was happening and walked towards me. I told him that I couldn't go on that parking lot. He pointed out a cemetery across the lot. It had been an Indian burial ground; the parking lot was paved over a part of the burial ground. As with any other cemetery, it was sacred ground...in this case turned into a parking lot.

One of my intentions on this vacation had been to help Pat sense spirits. Although she didn't feel too many things, once or twice she felt temperature changes in her hands. I told her that was an indication that she was picking up on the energy of spirits. I think she may have wanted to see them; I didn't. I see them enough; this was my vacation. After the tour, we went back to our hotel, and I prayed that we didn't bring any spirits back with us. I needed to get some sleep.

I had such an incredible two weeks on my vacation. I meditated each day and got messages from my guides, and for people I met. My wonderful vacation had come to an end, and I dreaded going home. As Pat approached the airport, she noticed three hawks above us and said, "Look, Gail, there are your guides...but why three?" I looked up, acknowledged them, and didn't give it much thought.

While on the plane, the pilot announced that we would be descending into Newark, New Jersey. I looked at my watch and noticed that we were arriving a half hour early. All of a sudden, I heard a male voice crying out loud. I looked around; most of the passengers still had headsets over their ears, watching the end of the movie. A few others who I made eye contact with looked surprised and concerned. I heard the crying coming in front of me and looked between the seats. I saw a gentleman seated at the window banging his head on the seat in front of him. He was saying, "Allah, I'll save the plane; I'll save the plane."

When a few of us heard this, we became apprehensive. I released my seat belt, put my ear closer to the seat in front of me, and observed this man still crying with his hands reached up into the air, claiming, "I will save the plane." I tapped the lady sitting directly in the aisle seat in front of me and asked what was wrong; she didn't know. I got out of my seat and spoke to the man, asking if I could help him. He looked up at me, with a glazed expression, and cried, "Allah sent you to me; I have to save you."

With experience in working with law enforcement, I had been in many case scenarios. The thought went through my mind that he could be a distraction and someone else on the plane could cause harm. I looked up and down the aisle, making eye contact with everyone who I could see. This gentleman proceeded to try to get out of his seat and I asked him to sit back down and put his seatbelt on. He still intended to get up, so I pushed him down.

When I had boarded the plane, I noticed two other pilots who were in flight. The one closest to me had headphones on watching the movie. I turned and asked a passenger to please tap the pilot on the shoulder to let him know there was a problem. The pilot came to me and asked what was going on. I explained that this gentleman had been yelling, "Allah, I'll save the plane." To my surprise, he said, "Whatever you do, don't let him out in the aisle." I wondered, *You're a pilot, why are you telling me this?*

We both stood in the aisle, blocking the man's seat. The gentleman became more aggressive and the only thing I could think of was to dive on top of him. I did just that—I dove across the other two women passengers and the man. Quickly I did a bodily pat search to make sure he didn't have any weapons. Still lying across the women, I calmly spoke to him, assuring him that everything would be okay, "because you are saving the plane." I wanted him to think he had control.

While I was doing this, he began to tell me of his personal life. According to him, he hadn't had a job for two years and hadn't eaten in two days. He said he only had one cigarette; he wanted to show me the box...but my guides said, *Don't let him open the box.*

As I began lifting myself off of him and the women, he started to get his cigarette box. I told him that I believed what he was saying; he didn't have to show it to me. He put the box back into his pocket and told me that he was from Haiti, had two children in Florida, his wife was sitting next to him breastfeeding an 8-month old child, and his other child was at his mother's in Newark, New Jersey. I kept talking to him until we landed.

Once on the ground, we sat there for a half hour. I realized that they had to secure the terminal to bring this plane in. As we continued passing gates, we were obviously being directed further away. I started to laugh and the pilot looked at me questioning. I commented, "Did you ever see the movie *Airplane?*" He replied yes...and then he, too, noticed that we were passing all the gates (as they did in the comical movie). He smiled and replied, "You do have a sense of humor."

At the gate, we were kept in our seats. When the door opened, the police stormed the plane and arrested the gentleman. Passengers and I in the immediate area were asked to stay on the plane for questioning. The flight crew, along with the extra pilot, thanked me for my "heroic" action in maintaining calmness on the plane. I smiled and said, "I'm really pissed off because we landed early and I'm getting home late." I should have been so grateful that all our lives were spared—the stupid things we think of.

I shared with them that if the gentleman had started reacting in mid-air, I wasn't sure how I would have handled it. The scenario could have been very different. Of course, I didn't mention anything about my three hawks forewarning me...and letting me know that everything would be okay.

## Look for the Dinosaur

As I began to feel more comfortable letting people know that I could see and hear spirits, word got around. My phone starting jumping off the hook; some calls were from people I knew and others were strangers.

Two men were out clamming (pulling clams from the water to eat) in the month of January when the waters were cold and choppy. The small boat was heading out the bay and fellow clammers warned them to turn back to the dock. They still headed out and while attempting to clam, water overtook the boat, knocking both men into the frigid bay. At the end of the day, they never returned. Family and friends went out to search, to no avail. Even the boat was gone. State police would not send out divers because of the cold waters.

One day I got a call from one of the men's relatives, telling me what happened and asking for my help. This person told me that their cousin had a 50-ft. fishing boat and was willing to take me out to search for Greg, the man who they feared was dead. We set a time and date. I must have picked the coldest day of the year; the waters had 3 and 4 ft. swells. Still, I went.

Greg's uncle showed me a navigational map; I had no idea how to read it. I gave numbers to the uncle and he told me from the navigational map, it indicated the site where Greg possibly went down. He took me into that area. On the back of the boat was a huge rake that they would use to dredge if I felt the body was in the area. When I realized that, I exclaimed, "I can't handle that – you can't bring up the body while I'm on this boat." They assured me that I could stay in the cabin; however, I was not convinced I could stay on the boat if the body had been brought up.

There were other relatives on the boat, although I did not know that Greg's father was among them. I started to hear Greg guide me to the area where his body was. As we got closer, they let the boat idle, dropped the rake and started dredging. When the rake caught something, the relatives said, "I think we got something." I cringed and pleaded with Greg, "Please don't let it be you – I can't be on the boat if you come up." They picked the rake up, and thank God, it was garbage.

**Dinosaur**

It was a grueling process. We kept shifting because the waves were so hard. Finally, I heard Greg say to me, "Look for the dinosaur."

When I heard him say this, I must have made a face, which his uncle caught. He asked, "What is the matter?" I told him, "Greg mentioned something about a dinosaur—look for the dinosaur."

His uncle got a shaken look on his face; then he told me that Greg loved dinosaurs as a kid growing up, and even had one on his own boat as a mascot. I happened to turn around, and on land, something caught my eye which was a piece of driftwood shaped like a dinosaur. I couldn't believe what I was seeing. We all stood in shock.

**Dinosaur**

I knew that he was trying to tell us his body was right where we were. The winds became fiercer, it was about 10 degrees, and the water was getting higher. We had to turn back. When a body is in waters like that, it tends to blow up from the gasses. Once the water warms, the gasses are released and the body comes up. In this case, Greg's body did come up in that area....near the dinosaur.

# The Animals Speak

Some people are able to accept the concept of speaking to deceased loved ones...but draw the line at the idea of communicating with animals. For others, the idea of communicating with animals makes perfect sense... while communicating with spirits goes *off the deep end.* Still, it's all energy, and Gail's love of animals makes her open and receptive to telepathically hearing animal communication. Nevertheless, it has not been an easy concept for Gail to accept; at this point, it continues to surprise her when it occurs.

When Gail speaks about her own pets, she introduces the reader to (a) communicating with animals, (b) being saved by one of her cats, (c) transition at death, and her belief in reincarnation of an animal.

◊◊◊

## Private Proof, the Talking Horse

While watching television I saw Sonia, the pet psychic. My initial reaction was to *poo poo* it, thinking that she was pulling the information from the pet's owner, rather than hearing communication from an animal. Soon after that, a woman came to me for a reading, wanting me to read about the trainer of her horse. She said that she couldn't find a separate picture of the trainer,

**Gail with Private Proof**

so as she ran out of the house, she grabbed a picture of Private Proof in the winning circle, which had the trainer in it. As I looked at the picture, I heard the horse say, "My front left leg has two breaks."

I made a face, saying to myself, *Am I losing it? Did I hear this horse talk to me?* Mind you, he was still alive. The owner looked at me and said, "What, what? Tell me what you get." I responded, "You're going to think I'm crazy, but your horse just told me he has two breaks in his front left leg." She nonchalantly looked at me and said, "Yes." I got up and walked away.

After I composed myself, I said, "But this horse is alive and he is talking to me." After all, I was used to talking to spirit guides or deceased loved ones...people on the other side. I asked, "Isn't it true that when a horse has a broken leg that you put him down?" Then I heard Private Proof say to me, "I'm a miracle horse and I'll race again." His owner said, "We think he is a miracle horse. My husband is a vet and he thinks these two breaks could heal and he may race again." This was so far fetched to me; this was not only one break, it was two.

My guides stepped in and reminded me of a friend who worked with healing oils and suggested that we use the oils on Private Proof. I thought this lady would think I was crazy. It was another instance where I had *poo poo'd* what I thought had been a gimmick. It was only after I experienced the healing properties of essential oils on my knee, that I understood their value.

When I told Private Proof's owner about using essential oils, I was surprised that she was receptive. I asked what her husband, a vet, would think. She said that she didn't care; anything that would help her horse she would agree upon. I gave the number of my friend. They set up a time and a date and I went to witness the process.

After 4 or 5 sessions of working with the oils, an X-ray was taken of the horse's left leg and it showed no breaks. I was so proud of Private Proof that I cried. What a beautiful horse he is.

I felt that I had judged Sonia and that God put Private Proof in front of me to realize that I, too, can hear an animal speak. My lesson was not to judge so easily and realize that not only can I communicate with human spirits, I can also communicate with animal spirits. I began to see that, without my suggestion, more people brought pictures of their pets with them for readings.

## Skippie's Story

When people make an appointment for a reading, I ask them to bring pictures of the living and also of the deceased. I had a gentleman named Ken Barnaby who had come for a reading and he brought a picture of his dog Skippie. *Oh no,* I said to myself *an animal picture.* I still struggle with the idea of my communicating with animals. But I was so drawn to this dog and I heard him speak to me. I knew he had crossed over.

**Skippie**

I felt the sadness of the dog; he told me he had a problem with his brain and didn't want his owners to have to put him down. He loved them dearly and was so thankful for all they had given him. It broke my heart to hear the sadness in his voice. So I had to think about how I was going to mention this without getting the owner upset.

Skippie told me that he ran under a vehicle to take his life. I asked Ken if the dog had been sick, and he said, "Yes." He went on to tell me that Skippie had encephalitis of the brain. I told him his dog was doing great on the other side and that he should know that Skippie had taken his own life, because he didn't want them to have to put him down. He did not want the owners to make that decision, so he made it for them.

Something had been on Ken's mind, so he asked me if I thought that someone ran Skippie over on purpose. The dog immediately said "No." Ken told me that the dog was struck and killed in his driveway by a visitor to his home.

Skippie went on to say that he was with Buddy. When I shared that with Ken, I learned that Buddy was his brother's dog. Buddy was still alive and it was good to know that Skippie was watching over Buddy. Skippie also mentioned he was with a German Shepard and gave a name of Nicco. Ken wasn't familiar with this name, so we don't know if Nicco is alive or has crossed over. To me, this shows that they also find friends on the other side.

Ken said that Skippie was 6 years old at the time of the accident and that they had treated Skippie like he was their son. Unfortunately, Skippie had been sick for many years and the veterinarians had a difficult time diagnosing his condition. Skippie had endured an MRI, a spinal tap and CAT scan with no clear diagnosis. He also had stones in his bladder, which had been removed twice within one year. The last 6 months of his life, Skippie had been on chemotherapy and cortisone injections. Ken shared with me that they had about eight thousand dollars in medical costs over Skippie's lifetime.

As Ken said, Skippie was like his son and no matter the cost, he kept trying to help him. Within the last months of his life, Skippie had shown signs of improvement, which can be typical for a pet which is getting ready to cross over.

Many of us go through loss of a pet, and the grieving process is just as bad as if we lost a human loved one. As I have found through many readings communicating with pets, sometimes they take their own lives not to put us through making that dreadful decision. I know that feeling, as I will tell about my own cat Buckwheat in a later story.

Ken shares:

*"My wife Michelle and I brought Skippie into our lives when he was only 6 weeks old. We treated him like a son, and he definitely knew his place in our family. He always acted more like a child than just a pet. We had a long rough road of sickness with Skippie, having taken him to most of the veterinarian specialists in the area during his life. Within the last few months of his life, it appeared that he was doing much better. Then one afternoon, in a freak turn of events, he went outside and ran to an area of the yard that he normally did not go, just as a car was leaving the driveway. My wife found him minutes later, and we rushed him to the animal hospital. But it was too late. He was here one minute and gone forever the next, or so we thought.*

*After a couple of very difficult months I contacted Gail for a reading, hoping she could connect with him. While I try to believe in spirit guides and the other side, I was more than skeptical about connecting with a pet. Once the reading began, I was instantly in tears as Gail began describing Skippie, his life and his ailments. I guess he is more than a pet on the other side too! We are so grateful to know that he is around us and that he knows how much we care for him. Nothing can bring him back, but if we know he is watching over us, we can move on with our lives, knowing that we will eventually see him on the other side. Thank you Gail for giving us affirmation and closure."*

## The Pregnant Horse

One day I went to visit Private Proof, the horse I wrote about previously. I walked through the arena that Kathy had for boarding horses. Mind you I am afraid of something so much bigger than me, and animals do sense when you are scared. As I stood in the arena another horse started to approach me. This horse was big. Kathy commented, "See if she tells you anything."

As the horse came closer to me I heard her say, "Will I ever have this baby (foal)?" I said to myself, "*Here we go again.*"

I looked at her; she didn't look pregnant, but then I had never seen a pregnant horse before. I began talking to the horse letting her know she would have that baby soon. She pleaded, "When?" I told her she would have it within a week. I learned that she was overdue two weeks...and any mother knows what it is like to be overdue, let alone two weeks. On the 5th day, the call came that the horse had her foal, and it was female.

About a month went by and I made another trip to see Private Proof. I was anxious to see how he was doing with his leg. I completely forgot about the new born foal. I got to the farm and saw Private Proof and he was doing well.

As I started to leave the barn, I again walked through the huge arena. Kathy and I heard the sound of a horse—I guess one calls it "whinny." We turned around. It was as if they had their own language; she took a few steps and all the other horses in the arena moved to the back part.

Then all of a sudden she went by her foal and turned around and started walking towards me. I didn't realize that Kathy left me in the arena, standing by myself. I can't remember the names of the mother or daughter horse, but it was an experience I will never forget.

I watched as "mommy and daughter" came closer, wondering, *What is happening?* The two stopped in front of me, the baby by the mother's side. I heard the mother say to me "This is my baby; isn't she beautiful".

I couldn't believe what was right in front of my eyes. I started to get all choked up and had tears. From the distance I heard Kathy yell, "She doesn't let anyone get close to her baby, including me." I was overwhelmed by all this. What could I say? I told the horse, "Yes she is beautiful and so elegant." Her shade of hair was so bright—a beautiful brown color that shined like no other I've seen. I just stood there taking it all in.

Then all of a sudden the "mommy" started to turn around and so did the "baby," right by her side. They slowly walked away to the side fence. The mother whinnied again, as if to tell the other horses it was okay for them to come back and they all started to walk towards the front of the gate.

### Raven

Joy raised Arabian horses and came to me for a reading. She brought a picture of a horse named *Wildfire;* however I was not able to connect with him. After her reading, she invited me to her home to meet all 16 of her Arabian horses. She was curious to see if any of them would speak to me.

I ventured out to her home and got to meet Woochie, a Belgium German Shepherd, who was the most beautiful dog I've ever seen, weighing in at 144 lbs. I felt an instant connection to Woochie.

Joy took me out to the barn. She had just finished feeding them hay. She took me to the stalls, one by one, introducing me to each horse. When we got to the third horse, she said, "Raven, come meet Auntie Gail." The horse looked up and locked eyes with me and I heard him say, *My back right foot hurts.* I must have had that puzzled look on my face, and Joy asked if Raven said anything. I repeated what the horse told me.

"He told you that?" Joy responded. She proceeded to tell me that when he was a baby, he got his right foot caught in barbed wire which did a lot of damage. They thought they would have to put him down. They called the vet in and he was able to sew the hoof back together. Joy's next question was, "Is he saying it still hurts?" I told her, "I don't even want to know." I still have a problem believing that I can hear animals speak.

Joy also told me that the injury is not visible to the human eye. Only she, the vet and the blacksmith knew of Raven's injury. She introduced me to the rest of the horses, but I know that I put a block up so that I wouldn't hear any more messages.

## Buckwheat, Stymie, Algebra: My Little Rascals

I was always a lover of cats and all my life had two to five at a time. I loved dogs too, but every time we got a dog, something would happen to it; either someone would steal it or somehow they would not last long and die. It was too heart breaking for me to continually go through this all the time. I had three special cats that seemed to come into my life at the same time.

First Buckwheat arrived. When she was given to me, I thought, *What a ugly kitten.* And, she would spit at me as I passed by her. Never having an animal do this to me before, I wondered, *What the heck is going on?*

A few weeks went by, and as I was leaving work I saw two children standing outside with a box that read, "Litter Trained." Curiosity got me; I looked into the box and saw four cute kittens. I knew I would have to deal with Buck (Buckwheat) if I took another kitten home.

My adopted mom, Delores, was with me and she said to the kids, "Don't worry, she'll take two." I thought *What? Is she crazy?* We walked away to have lunch and when I returned there were two left. They looked so cute.

Delores kept saying, "Oh go ahead and take them." I responded, "Well I could take one for Buck." She put a guilt trip on me and replied, "You can't take one and leave the other sister behind." Guess what: I went home with two kittens. I watched the kittens snicker at each other and wondered, *What did I do?* I couldn't take them back, so I had to deal with this.

They seemed to be settling in and getting along. I decided to name them Buckwheat, Stymie and Algebra, my little rascals...and that they were. They had their own personalities, as all animals do. As time went by, I noticed that Stymie liked to watch TV. It cracked me up because it was as if she really knew what was going on. If there was a ball game on, she used to try to catch the ball or chase it on the 47-inch TV screen.

One day in a mood to be alone and not bothered, I decided to watch a movie and took out *Snow White and the Seven Dwarfs.* I loved Disney movies for the kids and I was still a kid at heart.

While I sat and watched the movie, I noticed Stymie stopped what she was doing and came running into the room to sit in front of the TV. She intently stared at the screen, and seemed to like the movie as well. There was something about the Seven Dwarfs, I noticed, that she liked; maybe it was their voices or their movements, the way they looked—I don't know. I watched her as she seemed fascinated.

One day I brought the same movie out to show a friend what Stymie had done. When the movie came on, we both laughed. Once again Stymie heard the movie, came running and sat in a front-row seat. We couldn't figure out what was entertaining her.

**Stymie Watching TV**

120

I forgot about the Seven dwarfs until one day I brought it out again to entertain myself with the cat. I wanted to see what it was that drew her to the movie.

It seemed when the Seven Dwarfs were walking together to go to work and started singing "Hi ho, hi ho, it's off to work we go," I saw her ears go up and she went closer to the screen. I said to myself, *She likes the music, and perhaps the way they walk all behind one another.* So I rewound the tape and played the part where they started to sing. She raised her ears and her eyes dilated. I laughed to myself and said, *That's it; she likes the music and the dwarfs singing.*

So when Stymie fought with the others I'd put that movie on and I knew she was good for at least an hour and a half. I took a picture of her sitting on my couch watching the screen.

Algebra was cute; she had markings on her lips of what looked like lipstick all around her mouth. Today cosmetic surgery has come up with a surgery to have permanent lipstick on; well my Algebra was born with it. Algebra was a sweet cat—caring, sensitive and loveable. She never bothered the others, just went on about her own business. Algebra slept with me at night and always knew when I would be home. I'd see her waiting for me in the window. As soon as I pulled in the driveway, she ran to greet me at the door. She was very friendly to whoever came to visit me; she greeted them too.

And then Buck—she was the funniest cat. She took no crap

**Buckwheat**

from Stymie; I'd constantly be calling, "Stymie, leave Buck alone." Buck would pounce on her, but Stymie usually started it first. I always felt there was something special with Buck; we became even closer as we grew older together.

There were times I looked at her and saw my father. Some people say that spirits can come through animals, and I started to believe this. One day I was preparing to do

121

a reading and I sat at my table praying. Buck sat next to me. I looked at her and saw my father's eyes in hers. Shocked, I whispered, "Dad is that you?...and if it is wink at me." Buck winked at me. I almost fell off the chair.

I thought maybe it was just a coincidence, but anyone who knows me, knows that I preach that there are no coincidences. So I spoke to my Dad, kind of laughing, because when I was growing up my Dad was a little prejudice, "Funny Dad you come through a cat named Buckwheat." The cat ran away from me.

In 2000, I was sleeping as Buck came up next to my bed and kept hitting me in the face with her paw. As she was trying to wake me up, I kept telling her "Mommy is tired; I need to get more sleep."

I recall that it was about 4:30 am. She kept it up and kept crying so I thought, *Now you have me up; what is the matter?* I was so tired. As I started to walk downstairs I felt such cold come over me, and when I reached downstairs it really was cold. I looked at the thermostat and it read 50 degrees even though I had it set for 70. I wondered what was going on.

I went downstairs to where my furnace was and saw that no pilot light was on. The more I tried to light it, the sleepier I became. I recognized that it must be carbon monoxide and that I was in trouble. I ran upstairs, called the gas company and advised them of the problem.

They arrived in 10 minutes and told me to clear my home. I explained that I had three cats and had to find them. I had this poor guy looking all over my house with me for my cats. We did find them all and I sat outside in my car at 5:00 in the morning.

When he went in to use his gas meter, he found there was carbon monoxide in the house and tagged my furnace because it had completely broken down. I thank Buck because if she didn't wake me up when she did, we all might have died.

I took all three to the vetinarian that morning and told her what had happened. I wanted them all tested for carbon monoxide, so if they needed oxygen they could get it and clear their lungs. The vet found this to be a great story for the American Veterinary magazine, and asked if I minded if she put my story in. Of course I was so proud of Buck, and said yes.

The vet said she really did save me that morning, and I agreed. Animals do sense when there is something wrong and they do try to let us know, so when a pet acts funny or tries to get something across, it is important to heed what they are trying to show or tell you. It could actually save your life. Buckwheat saved mine.

I had the three of them for quite a long time. All the cats I ever had crossed over when they turned 12, so I braced myself, as they came closer to that age. I couldn't bear the thought of losing any of them. I noticed that Algebra was getting bad breath; I just thought it was something she had eaten. Time went on and a friend advised that maybe my cat needed to get her teeth cleaned. I noticed that they were yellowing and had tar around them, so I made an appointment to get her checked.

The day turned me inside out. The vet advised me that Algebra had a tumor in her lower jaw and said it was cancer. I became so upset and asked what I could do. The vet said I could go with surgery, but there were no guarantees. I instructed her to set the date, "Let's do it." I couldn't bear the thought of losing her. I felt so bad that I let it go for so long; my guilt was overwhelming. I prayed for her, and asked God please not to take her.

Algebra had surgery, and the bad news followed; she had maybe 6 weeks, or days. In that moment, I felt as if my heart would collapse. I took Algebra home, and held her as much as I could, letting her know I was so sorry for not paying attention to her. Then I realized she was trying to tell me something.

Algebra would come up to me and talk. I talked back to her and she continued to talk to me, but why wasn't I hearing her? All my friends got a kick out of her because she would meow at me as if telling me something and I would say "So how's the weather?"...and she would meow, meow meow. I would ask, "Do you love me?" and she would once again meow.

A month went by. I was working on my computer and Buck was lying down on the couch in my office. We heard a loud thumping. Buck raised her head and meowed at me as if to say "You'd better check upstairs." I went upstairs and I found Stymie in a seizure. In all the years I had her, she had never had a seizure. I picked her up and held her as I started to panic. I counted six seizures back to back. I called the vet and left a message on her voice mail. Within a half hour, she returned my call. I explained what was happening. She said to bring Stymie right in.

I had to leave her at the office for them to watch her and around 5:00 pm, they said I could come to get her. When I arrived, the vet came into the room; I could tell by her face that it was not going to be good. She said that Stymie hadn't had any more seizures that day, but that they had given her meds to calm her down. She then proceeded to tell me that Stymie had a brain tumor. Talk about shock. I cried and asked, "How?" *My God, I have Algebra home with jaw cancer, and now this.*

She told me that when they brought her into the room, I would notice that she circles to the left; that lets them know the brain has a tumor. She said I could bring her back to get a CAT scan but it would cost me well over a thousand dollars. I had just paid $900 for Algebra's surgery. I didn't want to believe this was happening.

So I took Stymie home with me along with the meds she had to have and stayed on the floor with her all night. In the meantime, I had a coffin made for Algebra, so I used that to keep Stymie in so she wouldn't move around too much. She was medicated and could hurt herself. The coffin that was made was large so there was enough room in it. So I sat, trying to work each day with the thoughts of losing not one but two cats at the same time. *Strange,* I said to myself, *they are sisters and now dying together with cancer.*

Stymie passed on November 26, 2001. She came to me at 3:00 am in the morning, with a howling cry that a cat sometimes makes when it is getting ready to go. She woke me up and I held her as I lay on the floor with her. I cried my eyes out not believing this was really going to happen. I fell asleep and once again she woke me up with that awful howl. I held her in my arms saying, "I'm so sorry that you have to go." I told her that I loved her so much and that I would truly miss her. I told her Aunt Ginger (my sister) would come for her, and bring her to the "Rainbow Bridge."

In my experience, *The Rainbow Bridge* is where our animals go when they cross over until we get there; then they come to greet us. I felt her spirit leaving and wanted to let her lay on my bed. As I put her down, I felt her come back again. I told her I was going to go downstairs and come right back up and that I would let her go with Ginger. When I returned upstairs in less than a minute, she was gone. I was a mess.

Now Algebra and Buck knew something was not right. They came up to my bedroom and jumped on the bed, slowly walked up to Stymie and then walked away. I covered her and waited for my friend John to come and seal her in the coffin and dig the grave for her.

**Algebra**

Three days later Algebra left me. November 29, 2001. How much can one take; two in one week? I thought of this whole situation and wondered, *What is my lesson here?* What my guides told me was that Stymie knew her sister was going to be leaving her and knew of the pain she was having. She didn't want Algebra to go over alone, she would go first to be the one to greet her when she arrived. I thought to myself, *Well I can understand that, but it still hurts so bad to lose the two back to back.*

Since then I have seen Algebra's spirit come for visits, not only in my home but also when I travel. Sometimes in a hotel room, I'll feel something jump on the bed; it startles me. I wake up and think I am at home and then realize that it's Algebra wanting to sleep with me still, even after passing. I do know it is her because of her vibration. I tell her that I miss her and that I still love her.

So, it was me and Buckwheat. We had each other, and we continued to grow in love. She was my side kick and never left me. Buck followed me everywhere and stayed on the bed with me when I went to sleep. She woke me up every morning. She purred so loudly I couldn't miss her.

Buck was now 12, so what was I to think: *Is she next?* I prayed so hard for her to stay with me a little longer. I felt bad when I had to leave her, for she was alone in the house. I really didn't want to get another cat. I just couldn't see me going through this over and over again.

Still, I knew when I was not home Buck was alone and I couldn't do that to her, so I sought out another kitten. A friend of mine said someone she worked with had a cat that had kittens, so I said I would like to have two females. I wanted them in twos; this way they came from the same litter and they could be together. Jeannie called me and said I could look at the kittens, but when I got there I saw the two that I wanted were already taken. I did not want a male cat. I figured it wasn't meant to be.

Another month or so I was called by Jeannie saying that someone took the one female cat but not the other; she asked if I was still interested. I thought, *Well maybe I should go look again.* When I picked up the kitten, I felt a strange connection. I felt like I had known her before, but couldn't quite put my finger on it. I took her home with me. This one was born on the day some say the sign of Aquarius went in, so I called her Aquarius.

Well Buck was not happy with a new cat initially, but eventually they became friends. I saw again something strange about this cat; she liked to watch TV. I looked at her markings and realized she had the same markings as Stymie and the same coloring. I know animal souls come back into other animals, just like the souls of humans come back in human form. As time went on she was into everything as a kitten would be and I started saying to her "You're a little stinky." The next thing I knew she was answering to the name Stinky, so it stuck.

I decided one day to play the tape of the Seven Dwarfs and guess what...Stinky came running from another room and sat in front of the TV and watched it. I really believe that Stymie has come back. She didn't take long—she came back in two months from Stymie, to Stinky.

Buck had been diagnosed with having a thyroid problem so she had to be on meds. It wasn't easy getting someone to give her medicine. She gave me such a hard time I couldn't imagine having someone else give her the meds.

I called a friend named Audrey and asked her if she could do me a favor and give Buck her meds while I was traveling. With hesitation she said yes. Well, Buck wanted no part of anyone giving meds. She gave such a hard time that Audrey had to bribe the cat with liverwurst. Buck seemed to like it so that was a step. Then she caught on to Audrey's tricks and tried once again to outsmart my friend. So now we not only needed Audrey, but her mom as well. Her mom sat on the stairway so Buck wouldn't run upstairs and get underneath the bed.

Once again I had to call Audrey to see if she could take care of my cat while I went away. This time as I was calling her, my guides came to me saying that I wouldn't need her to take care of Buck. *Odd* I thought, but called anyway. I asked Audrey if she could do me that favor; it was going to be in September and she was also going away. I wondered to myself, *Now what?* I was going to be away for ten days; who was I going to get to take care of her? Once again my guides came to me and said, *No need to worry.*

In July a friend of mine called and made a proposition about doing seminars. I thought it would be great, but if more travel was going to take place I couldn't always ask Audrey to take care of Buck. I decided to call the vet and see if she had someone who could do it. No matter who I called, no one could help me and once again I thought it was odd.

I had to take Buck to the vet. Thyroid sometimes causes weight gain or loss; in her case it was weight loss. I thought she needed to have her med's adjusted. So I took her on June 30, 2004. When the vet came in, I expected her to take blood, check the thyroid levels, and adjust the medication. But when the vetinarian examined Buck, she looked at me with the look I have seen before. I said, "No way." I knew right away that Buck had cancer.

The vet knew how I was with my cats; this one was going to do me in. I had told the doctor previously that if anything ever happened to Buck they would have to take me out in a straight jacket. The vet told me there was no option of surgery, and I lost it. How could this be; this was the hardest I have ever been hit.

I took her home crying all the way, as she looked at me through the pet carrier. I didn't want her to see me cry. I kept telling Buck everything was going to be okay. I asked God, "Why? I loved all my cats but why Buck?" The answer came back, *She gave you three more years of her life*. I realized that Buck had been on her meds for three years and at that time the doctor told me there was no guarantee how long she would live.

That night as I sat on my couch Buck came and sat down by my feet and looked up at me. The sadness in her eyes was killing me. I told Buck how much she meant to me and I couldn't believe this was happening. I heard her say to me, *You are going on a new journey, I do not want to be in the way, so I chose to go on my journey.* What she knew was that I was going to have a hard time getting someone to always give meds to her. This journey with the seminars meant that I would be traveling more than I had. So she chose to opt out of this life and go onto the next.

I cried so hard, thinking *Wow, she knows that my journey is now beginning to widen and she didn't want anything to get in my way.* As the days went by, I told her how much I loved her. I held and kissed and rubbed her. I had always given Buck Reiki (a hands-on healing) each morning. She would come up, lie on the bed, and stretch out. I massaged her. She loved it. I asked God each time I gave it to her to please let her stay with me longer, but it was Buck's will to move on.

The day had come. Buck came to me in the morning waking me up with a look in her eyes saying to me she was ready. I took her in my arms and held her saying, "I know you have to go but I will miss you so much. You need to come back and let me know you are okay." I called the vet and made the appointment.

I waited until the late afternoon so I could spend more time with her, and have my neighbor drive. I watched her rest and then took out the video camera 15 minutes before we had to go. I spoke with her as I cried and told her she had given me the best 15 years of her life and mine. I would never find a cat like her again. Each time I spoke with her she would answer me as if she knew what I was saying, and I felt she did. I told her Aunt Ginger would come and that she would see Stymie and Algebra and the rest of my family. I felt my dad come and I asked him to watch over her.

The amazing thing with her was that she answered everything I said to her, and I am so glad I have it on tape. I know she didn't want to see me upset. I kept telling her the love she gave me I didn't even get from my own children. She gave me the utmost, unconditional love. Anytime I was not feeling well, Buck was there, sitting on my lap and taking my pain away. Buck was so attuned to me; she was a healing cat. The time came to go for that dreaded ride, I wrapped her in a blanket; she didn't even flinch or fight me, as she usually did. At other times, she would hyperventilate, drool and carry on. All animals know when they are going to the vet's office; some like it and most don't.

In the room, she was like a trooper; she amazed me. She lay down on the table as we waited for the doctor to come in. Buck had a loud purr. I gave her more Reiki and told her my family would come soon to take her to the Rainbow Bridge. She looked at me with thoughts of, *I will be just fine; you go on that journey. Many need your help and strength.* I kept rubbing her forehead.

When the vet came, she already had tears in her eyes. She knew what Buck meant to me. She said "Mrs. Lionetti, I will never forget Buckwheat. Every time you brought her she would lie down and purr so loudly, even when I took blood, or listened to her heart. She said this was very hard for her too since she had taken care of Buck for 15 years. It was even harder for me to see tears in the vet's eyes.

She shaved Buck's leg for the needle. As I cried, I rubbed Buck's head, telling her it was okay and that I would always love her. She was purring so loudly; she looked up at me, I kissed her on the forehead and then there was no more purring. I went hysterical.

For those who have had pets and lost pets, my heart goes out to all. But I believe that they do come back, and they can come back through another animal. As we chose our families to come back to in each life, so do animals. I tell everyone to look in the eyes of their pets or look at the actions and they may see a resemblance of a past pet; they carry the same characteristics.

# My Feline Buck

Does she know she brings me laughter
With her silly idiosyncrasies
Giving pleasure when least expected
In such delightful, jovial ways?
Does she know she brings me mystery
In her puzzling stares at cryptic places
Are they fantasies of prey caught bodily
Or just indifference in her gaze?

Does she know she is comfort
When life's adversities cause pain
That she is in my haven in time of need
Whether I be right or much to blame?

Does she know she has the power
To break a human's heart
When life's journey calls her to another realm
And from here she must depart?

Yes, I think she knows these things and more
For love need not be spoken
It's shown in the ways we care for another
That build a bond unbroken.

# Working with Law Enforcement

Gail began working as an investigator, assisting local police departments to find missing persons. Initially the challenge was with people understanding or accepting her perceptions enough to explore what she was getting. After all, in some instances, she was hearing the deceased person talking as s/he led Gail to their physical body!

It appears that Gail's soul incarnated with a specific purpose—to use her psychic gifts to help others. Of course, she did not consciously know this until much later in life. Nevertheless, she (and each of us) brought 80% of the talents and abilities that are needed in order to accomplish the life plan for this lifetime.

Consider how Gail's life journey had eventually guided her to her "soul's purpose." From jobs as a store detective or security manager to working with inmates in jail, she was gaining knowledge and skills. Gail was being guided to a way that she could use her psychic abilities and serve others in need under the most traumatic circumstances. This type of reflection can be done for each one of us.

Our spirit incarnates and joins with the genes of our parents, our parent's parents, our grandparents' parents...on and on. We are a product of our ancestry—not only physical characteristics, but also cultural, religious and societal programming and beliefs, and mental and emotional states. This newborn infant, this "new creation" has never been on the earth before.

And yet, as you will learn, Gail's soul brought in painful memories from past incarnations that would inhibit her using that gift; she thought of it as "witchcraft." She would need to be pushed beyond that limited thinking to release the emotional charge that she carried around "witches." Those turning points came with two near-death experiences and meeting Helen, the psychic who assisted law enforcement officials.

Furthermore, Gail was born into a family which was not supportive. Her father was at sea and her mother caused enormous emotional and mental pain as well as physical beatings. As a result, Gail's anger built, but had no release until she began to bully her schoolmates. It all served a purpose; building that tough exterior would be needed in order to survive working as a prison guard and eventual private investigator.

She also had to reach the kind of strength that is needed to speak out about her psychic gifts – fight, when needed, to stand up for what she is getting from a spirit – and face the sometimes unbending law enforcement employees (i.e. police, attorneys, judges) that she would need to endure to do her work

In other words, our souls participate in planning our life's journey—it's called "destiny." Whether or not we accomplish our various intended plans depends upon us, our choices along the way—that is called "free will."

◊◊◊

### Charlie Chan and the Detective

A friend of mine had a niece who was missing and called to see if I could help the family. Nicole was last seen by her parents on March 12, 1993. She left the house with a boyfriend never to be seen again. I told my friend to have the parents call me and I would see what I could do.

While speaking on the phone with Nicole's mom, I felt Nicole come to speak with me; she was in spirit. I did not mention this to the mother, because that is something I just don't do over the phone. I asked her mom a series of questions and described what Nicole was telling me that was in her room. The mother went into Nicole's room and found everything I mentioned. I also described the tattoos she had on her body.

The mother asked me if her daughter was dead or alive, but as I mentioned I do not tell things like that over the phone. I just said to her that I had to work on this and get back to her, and for her to not let the detective on the case know that she had called me. I knew I would not get a good response from the police.

I called upon Nicole and asked her where her body was. She started giving me information and I wrote it all down. She told me her boyfriend killed her out of jealousy. Nicole wanted to break up with him and he wouldn't hear of it. At night, Nicole woke me up to talk to me. I told her I needed some sleep and that once I wake up it's hard to go back to sleep. Sometimes I turned on TV and watched *Nick at Nite*. She would laugh and tell me some stories. I kept telling her that I needed rest and to please leave me alone until morning.

This went on every night for weeks. She woke me up; I watched *Nick at Nite*. Later on I found out from her parents that Nicole loved *Nick at Nite* and stayed up late every night to watch the TV show. I thought, *How funny; it's as if we're both sitting and watching a favorite show together.* Nicole told me some things that both of us liked to do. I found it amusing; we had a lot in common.

I asked her mom when Nicole's birthday was and she told me November 2nd; mine is November 5th, both Scorpios. It reached the point that Nicole and I had conversations late into the night; that is when spirits are most active.

I asked her about what happened. I needed to get more information from her. She told me that Lou (her boyfriend) hit her numerous times in the chest knocking the breath out of her. When she bent over from pain, he hit her with a severe blow to her head with a heavy metal object. It snapped her neck and she died. She said there was a lot of blood but he tried to clean it up. He went to the 7-Eleven to get garbage bags and cleaning stuff to clean up the mess.

Nicole told me Lou had no conscious; he had done this before and never been caught. She proceeded to tell me that he cut up her body and then cut up the rug in the motel room and placed her in it. He then took her out of the motel room and put her in back of the vehicle. He made some phone calls for help in burying her; then he drove to New York and disposed of her in a shallow grave.

Nicole gave me information on where to find her. She said that she was by other bodies, there would be an embankment and a bend in the road, and she mentioned a lot of ashes and trees to the left with a funny trunk and bark stripped off...like a junk yard, scraps but not big. She gave me the numbers 70 and 726. She also referred to dark green metal, water surrounds, and she gave me the names Townsend and Tompkins and said to go by the bridge. Later I found out it was the Verazanno Bridge.

I decided to take a ride by myself, which I seldom do, to see where she would take me. As I drove to Staten Island, New York, she told me take the exit before the bridge, which was Bay Avenue. As I continued to drive, she guided me mentioning something about a smoke stack. I found Townsend Avenue. I made a left, that was the only way I could go and in front of me was a smoke stack. The street came to a cross street, which was Tompkins Avenue. *Hum* I said to myself, *she is directing me right to her;* I got a most eerie feeling.

I asked Nicole where was I to go next. From this intersection she guided me around the street and into an area where condos were being built. I continued through the area and as I got closer I really got the *hebegebes.* It was way back in a desolate area but I continued to move forward. I got out of the car and saw an embankment to the right.

I felt she was encouraging me to go down. I saw the trees she mentioned and there seemed to be some kind of fire that had taken place there. As I continued to walk, I saw a green metal car door which had the number 726 on it. It was getting more eerie and I sensed that it was not good. I felt someone was watching me but I didn't see anyone.

Where I saw the car door it did look like it was a junk yard, a lot of debris around, a dumping ground. From where I was standing, I could also still see the smoke stack. She guided me and I went down a little further and saw the bend in the road. Talk about scary. I was so frightened of what may be behind that bend but I knew I was not going to go there. I was walking in high weeds and I saw a pond (surrounded by water) and I saw a car in the middle of the pond. It was just about submerged but I could still see it.

I said to myself, *This is not a good place to be.* I told Nicole I had to leave because I felt threatened, once again as if someone was watching me, but I couldn't see anyone. I couldn't run fast enough back to my car. I got in, locked the doors, and got out of there. I sensed there was more than one body there. I went home and called the parents and told them I needed to talk to the detective on the case.

I received a call from Detective Bender and as I expected, he had an attitude like, *Okay lady what can you tell me?* It's typical of police since they have a hard time understanding psychics. I explained to him the information that I had received from Nicole's spirit and where I went. I thought maybe I could take him to the area. He said he would get back to me. I also gave him some information that I think made him realize I was on the up and up. All I have to do is give them something about themselves, knowing they never met me; that usually gets their attention.

Detective Bender called me back a day or two later and set up a time and place to take him where I had gone. He told me he would be in an unmarked car and to meet him at a parkway rest stop. When I arrived, I saw his vehicle but he was not in it. I knew right away that he was somewhere at a distance checking me out. I love the games they play.

So I parked my car and sat with my sunglasses on so he couldn't see where I was looking; I could play the game too. I noticed a man walking slowly up the walkway and knew right away it was him; after all he looked like a cop. He made me laugh. As he walked slowly by my car he raised his shirt to show his badge on his pants. I nodded to him, to let him know it was me and then opened my window and told him I was going to park in the commuter parking area; he could meet me there.

I got into the police car, said hello; then there was silence. To break the silence I said to the detective, "Your daughter wants to be in law enforcement, FBI?" He looked at me and said yes, I told him she would do well. I felt his energy change, and knew I was hitting home. Then I said a few other things and the tenseness started to lift. I told him some things about myself, so he would know who he was dealing with. I told him that this was not my case it was his. I did not want my name in the paper...or my phone number or address given out to anyone.

As we reached Staten Island the energies shifted and all was going well. He made me laugh, one of those tough guys, with attitude, but I knew he was a pussycat underneath. We approached the area and he asked me how I found this place. I reminded him that Nicole's spirit had guided me there. He, too, thought it was eerie.

As we got closer I told him I thought something was weird about this place, like someone watches. He laughed at me. We got to the embankment and I told him we had to park the car and walk down. He replied, "No we can drive down there." I asked him if he was crazy; he would tear the transmission out and we would not get home. He once again laughed at me. So here we go; he floored the accelerator and into the air we went, like Starsky and Hutch.

I told him not to go around the bend. I had a bad feeling with that, and of course he had to test me. We went around the bend and we both got an uncomfortable feeling. He started to reach for his gun on the seat, but couldn't find it. He asked if I saw it and I said no, so he felt around and I was sitting on it. He laughed and apologized because he got a free feel of my butt. (Told you he would be afraid when we went around the bend).

He backed up and then we left the car to go into the area I had checked out. He opened the trunk and got two shovels out. I asked "What is this for?" He responded, "To dig her up." I almost had a heart attack. I said, "No way am I doing that; I just came to show you where she is."

We proceeded down the area with tall grass and weeds, and Bender stayed behind me to watch where I was going. He was at a distance but could see me. All of a sudden I saw a very tall, well-built black man in the middle of the brush and got real scared. I looked up at Bender and he nodded to me that he saw the man also.

We continued to walk and I showed him the pond with the car in it. He noticed quite a few cars in the pond. Something was not right with this place; we both felt it. We decided we needed to get back to the car. All I could see in my mind was eyes watching us, yet saw no one near us. In the car, proceeding back home, we talked about the place and he said he would have to talk to the prosecutor's office about it.

The family called me to ask what was going on. I didn't want to tell them just yet. They wanted to get a cadaver dog from a friend who was an off-duty New Jersey police officer and they asked if I would be willing to go with him back to the area where I thought Nicole's body was. I agreed. They called me back saying the police officer would meet me by my house and I could show him where to go.

Well to my surprise, not only did the policeman show up with his dog, but so did Nicole's family, shovels and all. I had a fit. I could not do this with family members around; I thought *How can they dig up their own daughter?* No way was I having this. They insisted they were going.

I got into the van with the dog and the trainer. I explained to him that I could not do this with the family going; he understood and said he knew the family and would try to have them wait in another area to see if the dog picked up on anything first. I was adamant about them not being there and didn't even want to go.

136

We got into Staten Island and when we were at the scene, the dog was taken out of the van. Right away he started reacting. He ran from one direction to another. I was confused and asked the trainer, "What is the matter with the dog?" All the cadaver dogs are trained differently. The trainer said, "His reaction tells me that there is more than one body in the area."

That confirmed what I felt previously. The dog kept running like he didn't know which way to go. I looked at the trainer and said "We both know there is more than one body here; what should we do?"

After the dog ran into the pond, the police officer (trainer) said, "There are also bodies in the water. Let's get out of here." He didn't have to convince me twice. We were walking through very high weeds and suddenly saw a city bus in front of us. Someone must have stolen a bus and dumped it there. As we walked back to the van we also came across a brand new car engine, just sitting there in the weeds. It didn't take a brain surgeon to figure what was going on in that area. It was a dumping ground for stolen vehicles...and murdered bodies. We left.

From that time on, whenever I had to call Bender at police headquarters, I was to use the code name Charlie Chan. I told Bender that I loved to watch old Charlie Chan movies; he was a bumbling Chinese detective but the way he solved crimes was fascinating. So I used to love to call the police station and when they asked who was calling I'd say, "Charlie Chan." I could just imagine the look on the person's face answering the phone at hearing a women's voice saying, "Charlie Chan." That name stuck and I loved to hear Bender say to me when he picked up the call, "Heyyy Charlie."

The case eventually went to court. I was asked if I would like to sit in on the trial; of course I would. I wanted to see the murderer (Lou) up close myself and look him in the eyes. I just happened to be in the right place at the right time. The Sheriff's van pulled up where I was sitting. I thought it was odd; from previously working at a jail I would have expected a secured area when he was brought in.

The murderer was the only one in the vehicle. Lou was shackled and when he stepped out of the van, I was in plain view. Lou looked at me and immediately put his face down, as if he didn't want me to see him. I could feel he murdered more than once. He had a presence of evil around him, but I felt him to be a bit intimidated by me.

Once he was in the courtroom, I entered with the law enforcement people and sat among the victim's family and the police. A couple of times, Lou turned around and looked at me. I starred back at him and he looked down. I felt that I was reading his mind and that he was wondering who I was. It was good to know I had him guessing.

After all the testimony with the help from forensics to FBI, they were able to help convict the killer. Lou was sentenced to life in prison with a stipulation that he must serve a minimum of 40 years of that life sentence. He appealed three times and they were denied. Since his trial, Lou contacted someone in Brooklyn, NY and requested a hit to be put on the prosecutor. It was never carried out.

Nicole is at peace and watching over her family.

## Jerky and the Detective

I was working on a case as a private investigator and started hearing information that I wasn't quite sure of. Another private investigator, who we'll call John, was sitting in the car with me. He heard me mumble the words "face down, by water, white bubble, and numbers." John asked what I was talking about. He did not know that I was psychic so I commented that I was thinking out loud. As we sat together in the car, John kept talking about himself – what an ego. So, I started to tell him a little about himself. He looked at me and asked, "Are you psychic?" I responded, yes.

I kept writing down information. I explained, "I don't know where this is coming from, but I have to write it down." We talked a little more, and by the information I gave him, he seemed to think it was a case that another detective was working on.

John said he would make a phone call; he got Detective Barbara Stio on the phone. He told her that I was in the car with him, getting information, and thought that I might be a help to her. She asked me a series of questions and inquired where I was getting the information from. I said, "It just comes." It was easier to say that than to say it was my guides. She asked for my phone number and said she would get back to me.

A few weeks later, John called me from the site that he and Detective Stio thought I had described. They hadn't found anything. She wanted to know why I wasn't there. I talked with her and said,

"No one called me. Things have to be planned out; I can't just drop everything and go." I also told her that she needed to work with me directly, not have someone else between us on a case. A few days later, Detective Stio called me and we set a time and date to meet at headquarters.

We had had friendly conversations over the telephone, so I was shocked when I walked through the door and the first words out of her mouth were, "Oh, this isn't going to work!" My immediate response was, "Go f--- yourself. You called me; I didn't call you." (I later learned that she was under stress in an all-male department. She was frustrated because her bosses wouldn't let her do the job that she does so well).

I went into her office. As she took care of some paperwork, I observed her and thought, *feisty little one.* We then left the office to go to the area where we believed the body could be found.

Detective Stio (Barbara) barked at me to put my seat belt on; I told her that I didn't believe in seat belts. She demanded, "You're in my police car and I'm responsible for you, so put it on." I did. There was silence in the vehicle until she barked again, "And, don't you read me!" I told her that I wouldn't waste my time. We kept going back and forth, back and forth.

At the Palisades lookout, we got out of the vehicle and walked. The first thing I saw was the *white bubble* across the water in Yonkers, NY. It was the igloo-looking roof over the indoor tennis courts. As I stood there, I heard a female spirit begin to guide me to where she was. I walked away from Barbara and she asked where I was going. I told her that I was being told to look for something green on a tree. She yelled out, "All the *&^%^# trees are green!"

I proceeded down the pathway as she followed behind. I spotted green paint on a tree bark and heard the spirit voice saying, "over here," which led to a ledge on a cliff. I am terribly afraid of heights. I went to the cliff, looking down approximately 300-400 ft below me and heard the spirit say that she was straight down. I told Barbara, "She is right here; she is at the bottom of the cliff." She mumbled and we both turned and walked away.

Back at the parking area we met Sergeant Bradley, the dog handler for the cadaver dogs. I heard him ask Barbara if we came up with anything. She mumbled, "No, I don't think so." Sergeant Bradley walked towards me and asked, "Gail, did you get anything?" I replied, "Yes, but she won't listen to me." He asked me to take him to the site where I thought the body was. Once again, leaning off the cliff, I pointed straight down, saying, "She is down there."

**Gail with Police Dogs**

We walked back to the parking area. I wanted to meet the dog that would be working this case; his name was Baxter, the most beautiful German shepherd I had ever seen. I looked in the back of the canine vehicle and Baxter and I locked eyes. I said, "Baxter, we have to work well together; I'm your friend." I felt such a connection with the dog in that moment.

Sergeant Bradley told Barbara that he was going to go down and search the area with Baxter. He had to go 2 miles south of where we were, to a lower level, because the mountain cliff was so high. Barbara and I left the scene to go back to headquarters.

Back at her office, I met Barbara's sergeant. He asked if they took me to a few places if I thought I might be able to psychically pick up some things. I agreed. They took me to two or three different areas and I gave them some information and then they took me to lunch. I want to emphasize that I never get payment from law enforcement agencies...but they have to feed me.

After lunch and back at headquarters I was looking at some case files when the phone rang. Barbara's voice was astounded as she declared, "You're shitting me...and how do you know...and where?" She then stated, "We're on our way."

As we were driving, she told me that Sergeant Bradley found bones with a bra and panties attached to them, so it told us that the body found was female. At the cliffs, a few law enforcement people asked to see where she was below.

Once again, I went to the cliff, but this time could not go out to it as I had originally. My fear of heights had kicked in. I kept holding on to a tree and trying to lean over and point as they said, "Show us, show us." Funny how it is that the spirit seemed to take that fear away so that I could help find her – now it was back.

All of a sudden I heard a helicopter overhead and realized that the media listens to police scanners. They called out the prosecutors, medical examiner, Palisades state police, and emergency management. The weather started to shift and a nor'easter (weather very cold, rain mixed with snow and very windy) came in. Visibility was becoming worse by the minute. My concern was for Sergeant Bradley and Baxter 400 feet below because it was getting dark fast and they would lose all sense of direction. The huge halogen lights they used weren't strong enough to go all the way to the bottom.

I started to sense something was wrong with Baxter. I approached Barbara and asked, "Are they okay?" She advised me that they were, but I knew differently. They sent a bucket down with some water and a coat for Baxter, along with a camera to take pictures of the bones. I still sensed something was wrong with Baxter. Once the Polaroid photos came up and were approved by the medical examiner, she gave the okay to send the bones up in the bag being sent down.

I did not want anyone to know who I was. When I work these cases, I feel it is the detective's case, not mine. All are forewarned not to tell who I am. I always stressed that I didn't want my name to ever appear in the newspaper.

I was still concerned for the cadaver dog and brought it up again to Barbara. She said that I was a pain in the ass and yelled, "Go sit

**Detective Stio and Gail**

in the police car!" I sat about 3 minutes and had to get out because I still felt uncomfortable about Baxter. She told me that Sergeant Bradley and Baxter would meet us at headquarters but first we had to stop at Palisades state police, that all law enforcement were going to meet to go over what had just taken place. Then, she said they would want to know who

I was. I had a fit. I yelled at her, "If you give them my name, you'll never see or hear from me again."

At the state police headquarters I sat outside while all others convened in a meeting room. While waiting I viewed the missing children posters to sense which were alive and which were dead. The prosecutor came out, introduced himself, winked at me, extended his hand and asked my name. Dummy me, I gave him my real name; I just didn't want my name in the newspapers. He said, "Great job" and walked away.

Barbara came out, saying that we could leave, and took me to dinner. I asked once again if she had heard anything about Baxter. She said that we'd see him at headquarters. Once we got back to her office and I did not see the dog, she told me that he had been hurt. She knew what an animal lover I was and didn't want to upset me by telling me earlier. I later learned that Baxter hurt his spine in all the thick brush that was below the cliffs. It broke my heart.

She also told me that she was able to convince the journalists to leave my name out of the newspapers. When the article appeared, it was titled, "Practice ends as dog finds real body: Alpine exercise takes grim turn." [See article in Appendix]

I later learned that Baxter was retired because of his injury. He goes out on the cases to make him feel that he is still doing his job, although he has to remain in the canine vehicle.

A month later, I asked Barbara to take me back to the crime scene. I wanted to take pictures of how far down the cliff was for my own files. She took me to a very old house in the same area; she was curious to see if I could pick up any spirits. I was slowly walking behind her when she turned around and yelled, "Come on, Jerky, let's go."

I stopped in my tracks with a puzzled look on my face. She asked, "What?" I told her those words were exactly what my sister used to say to me in jest, "Come on, Jerky, let's go." At that moment, I looked at Barbara and saw my sister in her. I told Barbara that if my sister were alive today, she would have loved her. At that moment, I felt my sister was with us.

# Sal and St. Anthony

I worked again with Barbara Stio on the case of Sal Marconi, age 10, from New Jersey. His father had a visitation weekend with Sal and never returned him to his mother. I told the detective he would be found alive at the end of March 1998. I kept feeling that he would be found somewhere in Southern Texas, although I knew they were traveling all over that state. I felt the father was trying to stay away from big cities. I kept getting the sound of an "A" for the area they might be in. The name of Austin came in; however, once I looked at a map, I felt he would be south of Austin.

Detective Stio called me up a few more times checking on my thoughts. She reminded me that it was the second week of March and no signs or any calls from Sal or his dad. I reassured her that Sal would be found by the end of March, and it was only the second week.

Barbara knew how much I believed in St Anthony. She joked, "Maybe you'd better call your buddy, St. Anthony, and find out what is going on with Sal. On March 30th I went outside to get my newspaper and found a box on my doorstep. It had no bill of lading on it and I could see that the address label had been removed. I looked at the box, saying to myself, *Is there a bomb in here?* Being a private investigator I never know who may be pissed at me.

My guides told me it was okay to bring the box into my house. When I started to pick it up, it was so heavy that I had to drag it into the house. I sat on my couch just looking at the box. I was confused because I recalled the night before when I came in at 10:30 pm, the package was definitely not on my steps. I asked my guides again, *Is it safe to open it?* They said yes. I opened the box and it was a set of books called, *Mysteries of the Mind: Space and Time.* I thought *How interesting.* They were packed tightly and there were 25 books in all.

The books were brand new. I was certain that I had not ordered anything like this. Using my two index fingers, I took one out from the middle and laid it on my couch. A new book doesn't automatically open easily, and yet this one did. I noticed a small picture at the bottom of the page and thought that it looked like St. Anthony. I got my eye glasses and it actually was St Anthony that I was looking at. *How strange,* I thought. Sure enough it was a story about St. Anthony, how gifted he was, and that he was able to travel out of body.

About 10 minutes after I read this story, the phone rang. It was Barbara saying, "Sal was found and his mother is on her way to the airport to get him in Alvin, Texas." That was the "A" sound that I couldn't quite get, and it was 20 miles south of Austin.

I told Barbara about what had taken place that morning at my house with the books and St Anthony. I reminded her that I was right; it was the end of March and the young boy was found alive.

I sat down after that call and wondered, *What was that all about? How did it all happen...the books and how the page opened to the story about St. Anthony?* I often prayed to St Anthony; he is one of my favorite saints. Suddenly, I realized and said to myself, *Oh My God; he is the Saint for Missing Things and he worked with me in finding Sal.* I felt that was the reason for the books to come and my taking out that one book, having no idea what they were about. I felt that St. Anthony was letting me know Sal was going to be found. I always say nothing is a coincidence. Sal was reunited with his mom at the end of March 1998.

Seven years later, I still have never heard from any person who told me they sent 25 books to me. After the incident, I dragged the large box into my basement; I've not opened it since that time.

### Skeptics: The Tough Task of Working with Police

As I walked a trail for exercise one day, I heard a voice call out to me. I knew there was a woman from that area who was missing; I wondered if it could be her spirit trying to get my attention. I asked where she was and she guided me through the weeds. It was in an open area, set way back from the highway. In all the years I had lived in that area, I never knew that piece of land was back there. Mary Bell was the name she gave me, which was the missing woman. She took me to an area where she said she was buried.

I got an eerie feeling and sensed that hers wasn't the only body back there. I asked her a few questions to get more information so that if I notified the police I could give them something that they might already know.

I noticed a few bones in that immediate area, and I picked one up, not even thinking that I could possibly be holding a human bone. That action was totally unlike me; it's as if I was in a trance. There is no way that I would have picked up or continued to walk holding that bone in my hand.

When I got home, I placed it on my kitchen table and then called Detective Barbara Stio, in a different police department than where I lived. I explained what had occurred, saying that I felt there was more than one body in that area. I also told her that I had picked up a bone and took it home. She asked where it was and I responded, "On my kitchen table."

Barbara raised her voice at me, saying, "You should know better than that. It could be a human bone and evidence." All of a sudden it was as if I came out of the trance. I actually freaked out realizing that this bone was on my table. I put it into a plastic bag. I scrubbed my kitchen table over and over, thinking, *Oh my God; someone's body could have been on my table.*

Perhaps I wanted to avoid calling the local police department because I knew the resistance I would get. When I called the local authorities, as Barbara had advised, I asked to speak to the detective on the Mary Bell case. When asked who I was, I explained I was a private investigator, not hired by the family, but I thought I had some useful information for the detectives. They asked if I could come to headquarters. They called two detectives off the road to interview me.

There is always a good guy-bad guy routine when dealing with detectives. One acts like your best buddy while the other one tries to break you down. When I went into headquarters I observed both of these men; I realized one would not have a problem with my information (detective #1), but the other one (detective #2) would.

Detective 2 went behind a partition and I knew he was eavesdropping. I identified myself to detective 1, again repeating that I was not hired by the family. I told him about walking the trail and what I had come across. I handed him the plastic bag that had the bone which I had picked up. I emphasized that I felt there was more than one body there. He asked me what brought me into that area, because it was off the trail. I braced myself for the reaction and proceeded to tell him that I was a psychic.

His energy never changed, but I could hear snickering from detective 2 behind the partition. I gave him all the information I had gotten from the spirit that called herself Mary Bell. He seemed to have an open mind. I told him that if they were interested in letting me help them find her, we would have to work with the Bergen County cadaver dogs. I mentioned to them that I work with the Bergen County Sheriff Department on missing persons, along with others throughout the United States. I gave them numbers that they could contact to verify my credibility.

Detective 2 came from behind the partition and exclaimed that if they decided to do this, I would have to work with their dogs. I responded, "I work with nobody but Bergen County cadaver dogs—take it or leave it." I gave them a number where they could reach me in case they changed their mind.

Fifteen minutes later, detective 1 called and said they were interested in having me take them to where I thought Mary Bell's body could be. He said that they had made contact with Bergen County and would use their dogs. I later learned that the detective who called spoke to Barbara. He told her, "Gail said there is more than one body back there, but we're only looking for one." Barbara responded, "Well, you should listen to her. Maybe there are other missing persons who have been dumped back there." It is surprising to me that he just repeated to her that they were "only looking for one body."

The next day, detective 2 called and asked me a series of questions. He implied that Mary Bell was schizophrenic; his tone of voice implied that it didn't matter if they found her, that she was crazy anyway. I became upset and said to him, "How would you like it if she was your missing mother?" He raised his voice, saying, "Don't even go there." I responded, "She is someone's mother, sister, daughter, grandmother...she has to be found."

It must have been out of their realm to want to follow up on something like this. We set a date for me to take them to the location. As we rode in the police car, I sat in the back because I wanted to get a better read on the two detectives. The brother of detective 1, who was in spirit, came to me and said he had been in a boating accident, four had been in the water, but he was found. He gave me more information to pass on to his brother. Detective 2 was just plain hard-nosed; there was no getting through to him.

We arrived at the scene. Walking through the brush, I took them to the area and showed them where her grave could possibly be. They talked among themselves and I walked away. The two went into different directions scouring the area. When they returned, they both carried brown evidence bags. I asked what was in the bags, and they put them right into my face. The bags were filled with bones. I jumped back and grabbed my chest, *Oh my God.* I asked what they would do with the bones and they responded that they would take them to the medical examiner's office.

Three days later, the dogs that I work with, Baxter and Brownie, came to go to work. I continue to be amazed at how these dogs work. Brownie is given a signal and he runs the area to get the cadaver scent. Once he gets the scent, he begins to dig; that is the sign that a body is there. I noticed at one point he was rolling in the dirt. I asked the dog handler, "Why is he rolling?" He explained, "When the dog rolls, it means there are animal bones. When he digs, there are human bones." I learned that depends on how the dog is trained—each dog is trained differently.

They signal to take the dog away from the body and then give another signal to see if the dog returns to the same spot. This is done three times to verify where the body actually is. Brownie returned to the same spot, starting to dig all three times. That told the handler they were at the right place. Detectives 1 and 2 went to their car to bring shovels. That's when I run and hide.

Approximately a half hour later, they returned to the vehicles, but I noticed on the dog handler's face that something wasn't right. I asked him if they found the body. The dog handler responded with disgust, "No." I understood that he was being professional and didn't want to say more.

I was confused, however, and decided to go back to the site. The dog handler put the dogs back into the truck and waited for me to return. When I reached the detectives, they were still holding their shovels, standing and talking. I was surprised and disappointed to see that they had not begun to dig. I didn't say anything to them and we all headed back to the vehicles. I didn't say anything because the energy that I felt from them was that they took all of it as a big joke. Yet, they had taken my time plus that of the dog handler and the Bergen Country dogs without following through.

Since the Bergen County Sheriff's Department had worked with me numerous times with success, they trusted my information. Even though these detectives were willing to go to the site, I felt they really weren't interested in this case. It goes back to their skepticism in a person's ability to hear spirits of the deceased.

The next day I called detective 1 and told him I had some information that I was going to fax over. I emphasized that I wanted him to be by the fax machine; I didn't want anyone else to see this material coming over because it was of a personal nature. I told him that while I was in the car, his brother came through to me in spirit and told me he had drowned in a boating accident. There were three others plus him, but he was the only one found. I gave a few other pieces of information that only he would have known. After I faxed it, I received a phone call from him asking where I got the information.

I explained again that his brother had come to me in spirit while I had been riding in the back seat of the police car. I asked if he could verify if the information was accurate and he said yes. Still skeptical, he asked if I read it in the newspaper. I said, "No, when did this occur?" He responded that it had been approximately five years previously. How could I read anything in the paper from five years ago, remember it, and connect it to this man as his brother?

I knew it touched a nerve and said, "At any time that you want to communicate with your brother, you can contact me. It will only be between you and me." I never heard from him again.

## FBI

Most of my information does not come through dreams; however, there are some exceptions. I dreamed of a red and white plane that appeared to be TWA. In this dream, the plane went down. During that time period, any time that I flew it was on TWA. I was horrified and woke up immediately out of the deep sleep. During the dream, I also got numbers, but didn't know how to place them; I wrote them down and put them on my refrigerator.

148

I had a client come for a reading and she mentioned that she was a ticket agent for TWA at JFK Airport. I told her about my dream. Since she flies often, she got frightened. She asked if I saw her on a plane that was going down. I immediately responded, "No, you'll be fine." We continued with the reading and afterwards I showed her the numbers I had on my refrigerator, thinking maybe she would recognize it as a flight number. She did not.

Approximately a month later, a TWA plane went down from JFK. I was shaken when I heard the news. Of course, after any such occurrence, there is an investigation. The FBI questioned all TWA employees.

Weeks later, there was a knock at my door. I opened it to see two men in dark suits. They presented credentials identifying themselves as FBI agents from New York. They said they needed to question me about a few things related to TWA flight 800. I invited them in, scared as shit, thinking, *What did I do now?*

Since I was unsure if they were at my home to arrest me, I thought I'd better call my attorney, Bill. I advised my attorney that I had two FBI agents standing in my living room to question me about Flight 800. Bill's response was, "Gail, what have you gotten yourself into now?" I know that he detected the fear in my voice.

I put an agent on the phone with Bill to answer a few questions. When I took the phone again, Bill assured me, "Gail everything is okay. They just want to question you, but if you need me, call and I'll be there." Since Bill lives only 10 minutes away, I felt more comfortable. I invited them to sit at my kitchen table and offered them coffee and cake.

I tuned in to observe and feel their energy to see where this was going. I realized, once again, the good guy-bad guy routine was going to take place. This was beyond skepticism; they just didn't believe in psychics at all. They wanted to know how I got the information that I did about a TWA flight going down.

As scared as I was, I had to let these men know where I was coming from. I turned to one and brazenly exclaimed, "You'd better stop what you're doing; your wife is onto you." He leaned back in the chair and loosened his tie, "What do you mean?" I responded, "You're cheating on your wife." The *good guy* turned around and said, "I'm not doing anything," and I replied, "I haven't gotten to you, yet." At this point, I felt that we were on more equal footing.

They asked how I knew about this plane going down and I told them it came in a dream. They asked if in the dream I saw the letters TWA and I responded, "No, I saw the colors. I recognized the red and white planes because I fly TWA often." I told them there were some numbers that I saw in the dream...that I was going to get out of my chair...and take the numbers off the refrigerator. I explained that I didn't know what the numbers meant, but they could have the paper.

During this process, the *bad guy* kept re-wording his questions to try to trip me up. I smiled at him, thinking *I know this routine,* and repeated the same answers I'd been giving all along. I decided it was time for me to acknowledge I was psychic. Of course the *bad guy* laughed in my face. I came back at him, "Be careful of the green car." He inquired as to what I meant and I replied, "You'll know when it happens." He asked if he was going to die. My sarcastic remark was, "Well, if you do, I'll be speaking to you again."

Two months later, the *good agent* called to tell me this man had been in a very bad accident and it was a green car that caused it. I made a phone call to him in the hospital and said, "You have to watch out for those green cars." His comment was, "Thank God I'm alive and do you have any other good news for me?" From that time on, we became friends.

I got a call from another FBI office, this time in my area. I learned that the numbers that I had given to the New York agents turned out to be the seat numbers over the wing where the fuel tank had exploded. The personal experience of the agents and the resulting investigation, including seat numbers of the plane, resulted in more credibility to work with the FBI.

◊◊◊

Occasionally Gail is asked by a person who is psychic how s/he can work with police departments. She often discourages it because it is so difficult to break through the walls of resistance. It has taken many years of determination—as well as a record of proof—for Gail to have the trust and connections that she has today.

Perhaps more time and education is needed for people to understand how psychic channels operate. Psychic input is not 100% accurate...yet neither is logical thinking when it comes to solving crimes.

In the 1930s, in the Rhine Institute at Duke University, controlled experiments and other scientific methods were established to research and test the reality of ESP (extrasensory perception) or psychic ability. Eventually scientific research was conducted on remote viewing (gathering information from a site as far away as 10,000 miles). Only one out of a hundred persons who volunteered to attempt remote-viewing proved consistently successful. However, occasionally remote viewers could achieve reliability as high as 80 percent.

The results over time proved valuable enough that psychics were employed in intelligence gathering, although it wasn't until 1995 that the government confirmed their explorations.

The Central Intelligence Agency released an official report (*The American Institutes for Research Review of the Department of Defense's Star Gate Program*) on the Department of Defense's remote-viewing program. In a speech, President Jimmy Carter confirmed that the CIA successfully used a remote viewer to find a downed plane that had crashed in the jungle of Zaire that American spy satellites couldn't find.

The Star Gate psychic spy program was officially terminated in 1995. Since 9-11, however, some remote viewers have been called upon by various government agencies to use every tool available to locate and stop terrorist attacks.[4]

---

[4] *The Gift: ESP, the Extraordinary Experiences of Ordinary People – Stories from the Rhine Research Center's Legendary ESP Files* by Dr. Sally Rhine Feather and Michael Schmicker, St. Martin's Press, 2005.

# Learning About Death, Suicide and Abortion

Gail often says that there are no coincidences. Does that mean that there are no accidents? According to Gail, that is true...although she goes on to say that there are also cases of "interference." Because that seemed to be a contradiction, she and I had a lengthy discussion, in which her guides joined in. I'm not certain that we came to an agreement, but it doesn't matter. Such theories—unintended accidents or part of a greater plan...or free will versus destiny—will probably always be with us. And, as I find in most interpretations related to spirit or consciousness...there is no *One Fits All answer.*

I have worked for several years taking clients into the *Interlife* (the time period between physical lives) with intention to help them discover information about the "planning stage before this lifetime." Not everyone is able to reach that level of mind; however, for those who have been able to remember even a portion of the planning stage, it has been enormously beneficial.

During one such Interlife session, a client, who I'll call Patty, sensed that she was walking (in spirit) with her guide. As they passed a huge library-type of building, she could see through the windows that many people were seated inside carefully reading large books before them. At closer look, they seemed to be deeply engrossed in serious studies. Her guide suggested that she go in, and she responded vehemently, "Oh no, I'm not! I'm ready to go; I've studied enough and I'm ready to get on with it." Her guide simply nodded and they continued walking.

In discussion after the session concluded, Patty said, "My guide was suggesting that I needed to prepare more before this incarnation. I realize that I didn't make much of a plan for this lifetime. I was just so anxious to get back here. And, throughout my entire life (now in her early 60s), I feel as if I've been *flying by the seat of my pants!*"

It appears that some people create a plan that is rather "set." Others incarnate with less of a *pre-planned life;* this offers them the capacity to make choices based on his/her ability and readiness at that point in the physical incarnation.

While in the Interlife, a client is only able to receive information that s/he is ready to learn. Not everything is available; life experiences and lessons are ongoing. Some people view their "plan" as in a huge book with gold edges, an image often thought of as *the Akashic Records.* Others see the plan as a huge blueprint that they can step upon; some have seen an enormous computer that has stored the information.

Although clients have not asked, I can be certain that they are not to consciously know when death will transpire. Still, it seems that the *soul* does know when and how death will occur; that may not necessarily mean the exact day or hour. For example, a person in a hospital with terminal illness may choose to wait until family members arrive...or choose to depart when family members walk out of the room. Gail discusses death and suicide below.

In the case of suicide, my experience through regression therapy is that the spirit carries the mind, experiences and intention of the person at the moment of death. For one person (for example, a person who is over 90 years old with a terminal illness and in constant physical pain), the choice to take his/her life may be harmonious to their mental, emotional, and spiritual "selves." In such cases, the person's consciousness may leave with readiness and a lightness of spirit.

In another instance, a person may commit suicide out of a desire for revenge, anger, or depression and grief. This soul will leave the body with a *heaviness* that may cause the spirit to remain in a lower vibration (I'm not saying hell, I'm saying a lower vibrational space) for a period of time. Prayers for that soul, over time, can help to lift them to the Light.

◊◊◊

## Sudden Death from an Accident

I have a friend whose sister, Dawn, walked every evening for exercise. She was hit by a car and killed; her family donated her organs. I read the letter from one of the recipients, Hank, who received her heart. It made me cry. Reading the words of the family, able to still have their dad alive today by receiving Dawn's heart, was very touching.

When Dawn's family met with Hank and his family, after talking for awhile, they realized somehow a portion of Dawn's energy was present. Hank said he was doing things he hadn't done previously; however it was in a good way. Dawn had been a loving and compassionate woman.

Hank's daughters explained that after he received the new heart, he wasn't as cranky as he had been. Aside from the emotional experience of getting a new chance at life, he expressed his own emotions and compassion more freely.

Many spirits who have crossed over from sudden accidental death would like you to know that by donating an organ, you are giving someone a chance for extended life.

Spirits tell me that they want to explain that it is okay to use any part of the body for others; they are no longer in a body and it does not matter to them one bit what happens to it.

We here on earth do not understand how valuable the human body is, and that it can even be used to prolong other lives on earth. If someone dies in an accident, their organ parts could help other people continue life. That is often a lesson that we on earth can understand by embracing sudden tragic death and knowing the individual's human body is going to continue giving life to another on earth.

Those who cross over from a sudden accident, or with others in an accident, remember that it had been programmed and agreed upon in the "contract of life." They are surprised to find themselves on the other side, but know instantly that this was to be the case, and are excited about being back "home." They do not have a sense of confusion or doubt about what has happened. There is a certain knowing at the time of death that they are going home, and it was what was meant to be.

In instances of a sudden accident (individual), gunshot accident, or drowning, oftentimes before crossing over to the spirit life, a person knows how and when they are going to die. I feel that a majority of the time, this is the case.

In other situations, the energy from another individual can intercept your energy, and make a sudden change of events. This can affect your original plan with which you came to earth. A person who is suddenly stricken down from an accident knows that this has happened to them for a reason. Such events can affect not only those who were close to them, but also affect total strangers. In those cases, there was a very definite reason for their death at that time and in that manner. It can even go against their "pre-planned intention" for this lifetime.

## Suicide and the Afterlife

Numerous people have come to me with family or friends who have committed suicide. Many of us have been taught that if we commit suicide we go straight to hell; not true. I have had many spirits who have committed suicide come during readings to let family members know they are okay.

Spirits often express that they didn't realize the pain they left behind and it was hurtful to them, as well, to see their loved ones in such a state of shock and grief. It is sad to see the parents or siblings go through so much agony.

Many people have thought about committing suicide; I know I have. But what stopped me was my belief in reincarnation, meaning that I would have to come back and do it all over again. I certainly did not want to come back to my mother. Even though I have tried to forgive her, I still say, "No way do I want to live this life over again."

I have been asked, "Where do people who commit suicide go?" Some are concerned that we go to a place like hell. I believe—and it is my belief—that hell is here on earth. Suicide is wrong and there are penalties but that is from our Creator and is non-judgmental; our lives are ours. We are not condemned to roast in hell for our actions. We have a loving, understanding God.

Some spirits go to the other side very quickly and function well. Others need a lot of rest or healing and they do not readily communicate. I do not find there is any set pattern; I learn from what they tell me.

## Abortion

No woman who chooses abortion should carry any guilt. However, in my opinion, abortion should never be used for birth control, and I have known some people who do just that.

If you ever had to make the choice to have an abortion, you can be assured that the incoming soul was in agreement. Perhaps the soul even sent you the message to follow through with having an abortion. The soul knows the situation that it is coming into in this life. If you are having a bad relationship with your boyfriend or husband and things don't look like they are going to work out, then the soul sometimes makes the choice not to come in (such as in a miscarriage). Or becoming pregnant at an early age and knowing you can't take care of the child, it may choose not to come in. Abortion is an agreement between the mother and incoming soul.

We come in for specific reasons and we chose our parents. (Oh God I hate to think that). We chose what we are facing when we come here; it is all about lessons and soul growth.

In a personal example of my son's first child, I told my daughter-in-law, Jen, that she was pregnant. Her initial response was that she wasn't pregnant, although she called two weeks later to say that I was right. What I didn't understand was that this was going to be my first grandchild to be born and yet I wasn't excited about knowing she was pregnant. A month later I got a call that she was losing the child. Still, I wasn't upset. I couldn't put my finger on it.

On December 15, 2000 I saw my former mother-in-law, my father and Jen's grandfather—all in spirit—standing in my living room. My former mother-in-law was holding a baby in her arms and I knew that the child had crossed over. Ten minutes later my son called and said his wife had lost the baby through a miscarriage.

Then it hit me; I became very upset and cried, asking God what happened. Yet when I knew she was pregnant, I didn't have any emotion. I have always said that in time we do get answers. Another week went by and my son called and told me he wanted out of the marriage. There was my answer; the child chose not to come in.

◊◊◊

As Gail shared about her relationship with Jack, having an abortion was excruciating for her. Even with her understanding of the soul's agreement not to be born, there was anguish; she even referred to feeling as if she had "murdered."

This shows the vast difference between various aspects of our being. We can grasp and accept a concept at a mental or spiritual level, such as *the spirit of the fetus doesn't enter the body unless there is a soul agreement between mother and child.*

The physical and emotional levels, however, may have an entirely different reaction. Based upon society's teachings, parental beliefs, or programming from others, our conscious minds will react, along with emotional responses.

One of my colleagues did some limited and informal research around this subject. She conducted a class of approximately five women who were in the early stages of pregnancy; in each case, the woman didn't want to bring a child into the world, but was also against abortion. My colleague met with these women three times a week for three or four weeks. They meditated together, and each in contact with the early developing fetus explained why they did not want to have a child at this point. At the end of the four-week period, three out of the five women had had spontaneous miscarriages. The remaining two carried their babies to full term.

In a few instances, I've helped women dialogue with the unborn soul after an abortion. Sometimes a lot of healing is needed. Many years ago, a client, who I'll call Teresa, came to see me. She had an abortion two weeks previously and hadn't had any conflict around her decision. She was a single mother and, after years of not dating, had begun a new relationship. She did not see any long-term future with this man, and couldn't handle the financial and emotional stress of raising another child alone. Although her decision was comfortable to her, she began to sense the spirit of the unborn child around her...and her emotions were running out of control.

During the session, in dialogue with the spirit of the unborn child, Teresa was told that the spirit never intended to be born. It had come to Teresa, however, to help her. She told Teresa that she had become *too logical, too rigid in her thinking, and she had lost the ability to feel through her heart.* Between the hormonal reactions and sensing this child-like loving spirit around her, Teresa was pushed away from her rational mind to feel her emotions.

Another session occurred in dialogue with the spirit of an unborn child, which brought a very different result. Marlene came to me in turmoil. She had two children and was happily married. In spite of always using double protection during sexual intercourse, she was shocked to find out she was pregnant. The reason that she and her husband used double protection was that Marlene had been told, after her second child was born, that due to her heart and predisposition towards blood clots, she could never have another child.

Before seeing me, she had gone to specialists who confirmed the likelihood that she would not live through the birth. They recommended an abortion to save her life; she had to make the decision within a week. She didn't want to have an abortion... yet she didn't want to die and leave her husband and two little children alone.

If Marlene hadn't been a person who was very spiritually aware, I would not have even done an altered state session with her. She was calm and mature, explaining that she was trying to listen to her spiritual guidance as well as her physicians. In the session, I guided her into higher states of consciousness, to see what information would come.

All of a sudden, Marlene said that the unborn child exclaimed, "You promised! You promised that I could come to you...that you'd be my mother. You promised!"

Marlene felt that there had been an agreement, in the planning stage before this lifetime, for this child to come to their family. Nevertheless, she still had a very difficult decision to make. She did not know whether or not she would survive the birth. When she left my office, she had not made a decision. She planned to talk more with her husband and specialists.

I didn't hear from Marlene for several years...and frankly, was hesitant and uncertain about what her decision had been...or in fact whether or not she was still living. I was thrilled, one day, when she contacted me related to another subject. She indicated that she had a beautiful baby boy, now three years old...which everyone calls *The Miracle Baby*.

# Religion and Spirituality

Truth is always revealed through many different voices. We are reaching a point where psychics are saying similar things as today's consciousness researchers (near-death researchers and experiencers, and past life therapists and researchers). This information seems to correspond with ancient religious and spiritual teachings from various cultures around the globe.

In addition, people are beginning to realize that there is a difference between spirituality and religion. Religious institutions are created in this physical world to help people connect to God, by whatever name they call the Supreme Intelligence.

Most often, religious institutions follow the teachings of one of the prophets, such as Abraham, Jesus, Buddha, or Mohammad. There are rituals, writings, teachings, tools or artifacts, and beliefs that a person must accept in order to be a member of the institution. Religious institutions, of themselves, are neither good nor bad—people make up the rules and dogma that may be required of members.

Throughout the history of mankind, religious wars have been waged, each side convinced that "God" was on their side. Human beings have been killed by swords, guns, cannons, and bombs in the name of God. It continues today.

Spirituality goes beyond any institutionalized religion; it does not require a church or writings or a prophet, although many people continue to participate in church and read spiritual texts as a part of their practice. Spirituality represents the essence of who we are—we are spirits, living a physical existence. Some people find their connection to God in nature, some by sitting in deep meditation, some by reading spiritual books or writing, and some by looking into the eyes of their children.

During the early 1980s, there was an "awakening" of a huge number of people to expand beyond religious structures. These awakenings took place in various ways, including seeing spirit guides or deceased relatives, psychic awareness, past life regression work, mind-body-spirit connection, and near-death experiences. Today we see movies and television shows about angels, the afterlife, spirits, mediums, and psychic phenomena; this was unheard of in the 1950s. Our children and grandchildren are being born into a very different world that will gradually come to natural acceptance of what is still thought of today as "supernatural."

Yet, if we read the early teachings of the Christian church, as well as other religions, we will learn that spirit communication, angels, prophetic dreams, and visions have always been a part of "religion." This is the way of the spirit.

◊◊◊

## Judged by the Church

We've been taught that we'll be judged by God on judgment day. Through my own near-death experience, the day that I crossed over, I stood in judgment of myself...and learned that God does not judge. We judge ourselves.

I have come to believe that all religions have been created by man to give us a foundation to live our life. What disturbs me is the brainwashing that comes with it.

While in the Bahamas, I met a young man named Oscar; he was a Seventh-day Adventist. We became good friends, and after several years I invited him to the States to show him the life that I lived. I welcomed him and several of his friends into my home. I enjoyed taking them out, showing them the sites, and buying some clothes for them.

Time passed, and I hadn't seen him for ten years, because he had moved to Switzerland, so I was so happy to have him fly in for my 50th birthday party. A lot of law enforcement people who I worked with were also in attendance. They stood up, sharing their stories about me and the cases in which I psychically worked with them.

It seemed the days following my party I felt an energy shift within Oscar. Because people in the Bahamas are very religious, I asked him what he thought about what he had heard. He told me he did not believe in what I did, and in so many words, that "the Bible teaches that it is the work of the devil." I responded that it was a gift given to me by God, and, as he knows, I had helped many people, including him. When he left to return to Switzerland, I gave him $200 as a gift for the arrival of his new baby and paid half his airfare.

When Oscar didn't communicate with me any more, I was

deeply hurt and saddened. I e-mailed, saying, "You have known me all these years, and know what I've done for others. You know I believe in God, yet you judge me through what you were taught. You accepted the money, and everything that I gave you and did not judge me as evil then; why are you judging me now?" I never heard from him again, and it continues to hurt.

## A Born-Again Comedian

In the last few years, as previously mentioned, I have had the opportunity to meet many celebrity comedians. In this writing all the names have been changed. Bill, who I had seen on TV made me laugh so hard that when I heard that he would be coming into town I made sure I went to see him. This man is so talented. He uses different characters for his show, real-life people who he dealt with when growing up; some were teachers and others were friends.

The first night that I saw him on stage, I noticed the spirit of legendary comedian, Red Skelton, standing on stage with him. He was dressed in the hobo outfit that he played as Freddy the Freeloader on television.

I saw another man along side of Bill and asked who he was. This gentle spirit said he was Bill's grandfather. He told me how proud he was of his grandson in making people laugh. However, I felt that this spirit had sadness in his heart. *How strange,* I thought as I again looked at Skelton dressed as the sad-faced hobo, *there is sadness in spite of Bill's comical act.*

About 3 months later I saw in the paper that Bill was coming back to the Comedy Club. I decided to go again to see him and this time to write him a note about seeing his grandfather on stage with him while he performed. I used my private investigator's letterhead, hoping that it would help so this man didn't think I was some "kook". I also wrote that I saw Red Skelton with him. There had to be a reason why Red was with him, but at that time I hadn't figured it out.

That evening at the Comedy Club as I turned in my ticket, I asked to see the manager and told him I needed to get the note to Bill. He took it and said he would do that. In the note, I had explained who I was and what I do and that I thought it was so nice to be able to converse with his grandfather and share that he was so proud of his grandson. I explained to him about seeing Red Skelton and said I had no idea why he would be in spirit on stage. My main reason in getting him the note was to let him know how proud his grandfather was of him.

The very next day I was surprised to get a call from Bill's wife. Mary said Bill was amazed to read what I wrote. I was curious about the Red Skelton vision and asked her why he would have appeared on stage. "Well," she told me, "Bill always admired Red for what he did in the comedian's world; he was his mentor."

*That explains it,* I thought. It was great to see Mr. Skelton because, as a child, I loved to watch all the characters he played on TV. Mary and I talked for over an hour. She shared some things about Bill and his childhood, many of which were not good. My heart went out to him and her. I explained my gift and how I only use it to help others. I wanted her to know once again that I was not trying to pry into their private life.

I've met many celebrities; I respect their privacy and never ask them for anything, such as autographs or pictures taken with them. I wouldn't want that done to me.

Mary said she believed in what I do, yet she mentioned that she and Bill were born again Christians. I said to myself, *here we go again; they are taught spiritual people doing work like I do are really helping the devil.*

Nevertheless, I did feel good about what we shared with each other and hoped that maybe they would not judge me. Mary even told me that she had gone to psychics; she recognized some were good and others were not.

I told Mary that the next time Bill came back into New Jersey, I would love to have the opportunity to meet him and share the story with him personally, but did not want to infringe on his personal life. She said she would set that up for me. She even offered comp tickets, which I declined because he has to make a living. I felt that I could not take anything for free.

The next time Bill came to town, I called for tickets including one for my son, Vinny, who loved this comedian. At the time Vinny was going through a sad period in his life. When we arrived at the Comedy Club, I told the manager to let Bill know I was there, as instructed by his wife. While sitting and waiting with much anticipation, the manager came over and said that Bill was waiting for me. The look on my son's face was a gift in itself. I said, "Vinny, come on, you are going to meet him personally."

We went to the Green Room, as they call it, and were welcomed. Vinny was able to talk to Bill and asked a few questions about how he came up with the characters he talked about in his show. We both told Bill how much we loved his comedy and to keep up the great work.

When I mentioned what his grandfather said, I could see tears well up in his eyes. Bill told me that his grandfather was his inspiration growing up and how much he missed him. I reminded him that his grandfather was with him more than he knew. I also mentioned about Red Skelton and he talked highly of him. He said that he loved Red and that, as a child, he too had watched him on TV. He had been his mentor for comedy. Bill felt honored that Mr. Skelton would be by his side. We told him we didn't want to take up any more of his time and wished him a great show.

Once Bill came on stage, I watched my son during the entire performance. You don't have to be psychic to pick up on your child's sadness, and yet I saw tears of laughter streaming down his face from Bill's jokes. Whatever he was going through, I felt happy for him at that moment.

When I got home that night I thought about Bill. Seeing what he went through as a child, was painful. My heart went out to him. No matter what struggles he had, he found a place to make others happy.

I received a beautiful letter from Mary, I have it framed and hanging on my "Wall of Fame." She spoke of how I am doing God's work and that no matter what crosses we bear God will always carry us. So true. [See letter in Appendix].

In the letter, she seemed to be saying that I have a gift, that I'd only scratched the surface, and that it is for a greater purpose. Even though both of them were born-again Christians, Mary was more understanding and accepting of my psychic abilities.

We continued to correspond back and forth, and then my feelings were hurt. Mary advised me that Bill was afraid that if his church found out she was communicating with me, "the psychic," they would ask him to leave the church.

I was upset to hear of such a stupid thing. I thought, *How can a church be so controlling? How can they judge others?* She apologized for having to tell me this, but he insisted that she stop speaking with me, and she did. I felt bad for her because in her voice I heard she would not have done this to me; she believed in what she believed and didn't let that interfere with the friendship we were beginning to have. Once again the teachings of a church—brainwashing in my opinion—showed its ugly face.

Because of that reaction, I have chosen to not see Bill again on the stage. I was recently at the Comedy Club and saw he was appearing; the management asked me if I was coming to see him and I said no. They were somewhat surprised but I didn't go into the reason.

## Going Beyond the Programming

Sometimes, people are more ready to go beyond their religious programming. A Jewish woman, who I'll call Mrs. Levy, came to see me. In beginning her reading, I immediately had a vision of a gun and described it to her. She was shocked and started to cry, explaining to me that her son had taken his own life. Her son's spirit told me that he would send her ladybugs, and when she got them, she would know they had come from him.

At the end of the reading, Mrs. Levy told me that she was a born again Christian. I asked, "What brings you here?" Their perception is that my gift comes from the devil. She responded, "I don't fully believe everything I'm told; I try to keep an open mind." She left feeling comforted that her son was doing well on the other side.

Mrs. Levy's daughter had made a trip to Italy, and during Hanukkah gave her mother a gift which she had purchased. When Mrs. Levy opened the gift, it was a bracelet of ladybugs. She later told me that she screamed out loud at the shock. Her daughter, completely puzzled, asked what was wrong. She proceeded to tell her daughter that she had come to me for a reading and her son came through and told her that he would send ladybugs...and when it happened, she would know they were from him. After the holidays, she called me to share what had taken place and to show me the bracelet.

I've had my own struggle with religious programming. In preparing a will, I had instructed that I have a funeral mass at Holy

Family Church. Upon speaking to a former nun of that church, she suggested that I talk to the priest in charge, since I was not registered in that church.

I made an appointment to talk to the priest and told him what my wishes were. He asked if I was registered in his church and I explained that I was registered at St. Ann's church because my children had to make their sacraments there. It was necessary to register in the church of the area where we lived. I told him that whenever I went to church, I came back to Holy Family; that was the church I grew up in.

The priest told me I could not have my funeral mass there unless I cancelled my registration at St. Ann's and registered at Holy Family. I got upset, and said, "As I grew up, I was taught that no matter what Catholic Church I went into, I would be welcomed because it was God's home. If I was in Florida or Massachusetts, no matter where I went, it was God's home."

I emphasized that if it was all about the envelopes (money) that they could send me the package of envelopes, but when I came to church, the envelope would be empty; I would put the money in the basket so no one could judge me by what was in the envelope. I asked the priest "Is that what it's all about—money?" His only response was that they could not do my funeral mass there unless I registered in the church. I chose not to register there, and not to return to that church.

My frustrations continue. When my children were baptized, we were asked to give a donation based upon what the family could afford. Now the church dictates what the donation must be. To me, a donation is what a person can afford; however, although the church continues to call it a "donation," there is a required fee for Confarternity of Christian Doctrine (CCD), marriages, and baptisms.

Even with my disappointments and frustration with the church, I still consider myself a Catholic.

# Seek and Ye Shall Find

When we truly desire to find an answer and to understand or learn, we are supported by the Universe. The answers might not come in our preferred timing; still, they will come. For Gail, the answer to *why does mommy hate me?* would not come until later in life. As an adult, when she was better-equipped to grasp their implications, her real search would begin.

One important answer involved a situation of Gail's mother which existed before Gail was born. Other answers came from an exploration into past lives. Gail's mother (and also Gail) carried unresolved soul memories from past incarnations when they had been together.

Whether you view Gail's past life memories as actual memories or a metaphor from her unconscious is not important. It was information that went from Gail's unconscious mind to her conscious mind, giving an opportunity for release and healing.

When I give talks, I like to explain that past life recall can come from different *energy bodies* that exist within us. We do not all operate in the same way. Memories are perceived in different ways...and, of course memory is not perfect. Past life recall may be:

- actual recall of a past incarnation of the soul,
- a metaphor from the unconscious,
- a combination or overlapping of past life recall and current life input,
- tapping into what Carl Jung referred to as the "collective unconscious,"
- a spiritual DNA that has yet to be discovered,
- fantasy coming from the personality or ego.

What is important is (1) the client's inner experience and sense of truth validating their current life experiences, (2) release of emotional and mental energy from the "darkness" of the unconscious to the "light" of the conscious mind, and (3) whether or not healing has taken place...whether the person is changed as a result of the experience.

In addition, if the past life memory appears to be "real," there are footprints. Some of those footprints may be validation of dates, history, or details.[5] Other times the footprints are more subjective and personal. For example, Gail referred to her Mother as a "witch" on several occasions. It also helps to explain why Gail—in spite of her psychic abilities—perceived them as "witchcraft." She kept her gifts secret, fearful of the reaction of others.

◊◊◊

## Answers to My Mother's Anger Towards Me

### Past Life Reasons

I would never have thought of doing past life regression until Jeffrey Ryan came into my life, so I don't know if I was a "true believer," or not. It seems to be a contradiction; I knew that we came back...but I hadn't realized that we come back from other lives. My thoughts had been that we crossed over into spirit and then returned. I had never connected to the concept of returning with memories of other lives. In fact, now I think that I probably wanted to block them.

After having a reading, a female minister mentioned me to her therapist, Jeffrey Ryan. She shared the reading and he said he would like to meet me. She called and gave me the message that I was to call him. My response was, "If he wants to meet me, he should call me."

Nevertheless, one night while at work, I felt prompted to call him. With a 100 to 1 chance, he answered the phone at 8:00 pm. I introduced myself. His reply was, "When are you going to get rid of the baggage with your mother?"

Of course I was a bit in shock...and told him I wasn't carrying any baggage with my mother. In reality, I had a truckload. I invited him to my meditation group as a guest speaker, talking about past lives.

I found it so interesting that eventually I began going for one-on-one sessions. At the time, I had no idea what it would entail. However, at the end of the first regression, I was in awe.

---

[5]Note: Validations of dates and details after a past life regression is still not proof of reincarnation; it does not prove that it was the same soul.

Jeff put me into a hypnotic state and I went back in memory to the 1700s. I was a young female, 15 years old. It seemed as if the townspeople didn't like me, and I didn't understand it. They spit on me, saying that I was "unworthy." Jeff told me to get away from the town and to go find my mother.

It appeared that my mother had a store with my grandmother; in this store they seemed to be dressed like witches. I didn't like the feeling that I got when I went into the store. Jeff told me to look around and describe what I was seeing. I described a big black caldron in back of the store. My mother was stirring the caldron. He had me step up and look into the caldron; I saw human heads floating. He had me step away and go to find a place where I would be happy.

I went to the water, where I could find peace. I sat there for awhile before he told me to go back into the town. As I approached the town, I had an over-whelming feeling that something bad was going to happen. I saw a huge rock in the middle of the town square. Once again, I saw people spitting on me. Then some townspeople grabbed me and put me on the big rock. They lined up on each side of the rock, stones in their hands. I kept crying, wondering, *Why are they going to take my life; I've done nothing wrong...I was a good person.*

I felt they were sacrificing me for all the wrongs that my mother did. They proceeded to put stones on my chest; they were becoming heavier and heaver. I couldn't breathe. I know I was fighting to save my life, but I remembered Jeff saying, "Accept your death and go to the Light." Once I started to lift out, I felt only peace.

In talking about it afterwards, I was confused as to why they went after me instead of my mother. It seems that they wanted to sacrifice me in order to teach her a lesson. [During the writing of this section, Janet added, "Perhaps a reason why they went after you instead of your mother is that the townspeople were afraid of her; they weren't afraid of you"].

When I left Jeff's office, I became angry again, thinking, *She won again.*

Over a period of time, I did several past life regressions with Jeff. The lifetimes with my mother showed, again and again, the relationship that was carried over from the past into this life.

> Once again, in a town square that seemed to be in Plymouth, Massachusetts, I saw myself as female dressed in an outfit similar to a pilgrim. I saw a guillotine in the middle of the town square. It amazed me how many people came out of nowhere to witness my getting guillotined; it was as if they thrived on violence.
>
> When I tried to understand why this was happening to me, once again I heard, "...to teach your mother a lesson." I never knew what she did that caused the townspeople to be so angry.

◊◊◊

> I was a female child, 8 years old. Although my life didn't seem so bad, I suddenly saw and felt activity in the town where I lived. A tall man with salt and pepper hair came to get me. He had on a white shirt, charcoal grey pants and old black boots that were well worn. He guided me into a barn to hide. I crouched behind the haystacks, listening to the voices outside. I couldn't quite make out what they were saying with all the activity, hustle and bustle. The man had to leave, and assured me that I would be okay and to stay where I was.

I heard the townspeople getting closer to the barn, as if they were looking for me. I tried to be still. I heard them coming into the barn, saying, "I bet she's in here." I was alone and so frightened, yet I knew I could not call for my mother. Three men found me; they grabbed me like I was a rag doll. I began crying, screaming and kicking. They took me to the town where I saw a make-shift cross. They tied me to the cross. I looked at everyone, asking once again, "Why are you doing this to me?"

People, including females and children, spit on me, telling me I was unworthy and that I was nothing. They proceeded to light a stick with cloth on it, then light the hay at the bottom of my feet.

These very similar past life memories with my mother helped me to understand the deep feeling that I had throughout most of this life. I always felt "unworthy," and my mother reinforced that feeling.

The way that I knew that my mother in these past lives was the same soul as my mother in this life is that she always looked the same. Her facial features and look of unhappiness in the past life was very much like she looked in this life.

◊◊◊

As Gail recognizes, the three past lives that she explored were very similar. Sometimes that occurs, other times the lifetimes one visits are quite different. It appears that if issues are unresolved, a pattern is created within the energy field (e.g. belief in victim hood, abandonment, issues of power, etc.) that keeps repeating over and over until it is released. Gail is working hard in this lifetime to try to release the stored anger, and to raise her own self esteem and move beyond the energy of victim, and to find forgiveness for her mother.

We can recognize a person in a past life regression as one who is in this life through a variety of ways:

- Sometimes the person recognizes them immediately (*Oh, that little boy is my grandmother in this life!*), even though the gender, age, and culture may be different. They are recognized through sensing the energy field; occasionally the eyes are similar.
- Other times, the person does not recognize anyone while in the regression, until I take them into higher realms of consciousness. From that perspective the person may have greater clarity: *Oh, the little boy is my sister in this life.*
- We do not necessarily know every person in a past life as someone in our current lifetime.
- I've also had people drive home and then call me, saying something like, *Oh, now I know who killed me in that past life.*

In Gail's case, remembering the past lives with her mother fueled her anger. Of course, the reason is that she was still carrying anger, both from childhood and from soul memories. Regression therapy brings forward memories in order to heal them. Sometimes the healing is instantaneous and there is resolution by the time a client leaves the office. In other cases, much more work and time are needed.

◊◊◊

In many ways, going through the past lives brought up my anger once again. I felt as if I'd always been victimized by her. Yet, I began to consider, as I explored the past life memories, that my mother had her own issues. I began to see that she tried to do the best that she could in raising her children. Just as my anger kicks up, I was sure that her anger kicked up as well.

I continued to work with Jeff over a period of years. He regressed me into my childhood in this lifetime. I was able to see that there were a lot of issues that my mother had with her own mother; I remembered her being very angry with her mother. I began to understand more—my grandmother died when my mother was around 12 years old. Her father had already crossed over, so her brothers had to go out to work and she had to become the "mother" in the house.

I tried to comprehend that it wasn't easy for her growing up. She lost both of her parents at a young age; it put a lot of responsibility on her as a child. She had it hard. I acknowledged that even after she got married, she was often alone since my father was at sea.

In trying to figure out what she had gone through in life, I meditated and called upon her. In a previous meditation with Jeff, she had told him, "Gail doesn't know what went on behind closed doors." In my meditation, I went back to the house where we lived. I could sense my parents in their bedroom and tried to open the knob on the bedroom door. I couldn't open it, and sensed that I wasn't supposed to see what was going on.

It would be several years later, when I visited the house where I grew up. When I walked by their bedroom, I had a vision of my mother sitting on the bed. It appeared that she was crying and my father backhanded her across her face. In reality, I never saw him ever hit her...and he never raised a hand with any of his children. Still I can accept that I didn't know what *went on behind closed doors.*

The greatest pain for me is the fact that the patterns continue. Whatever anger she carried—whether from past lives or the current life—it affected her so strongly. She refused to connect to family; she constantly created rifts between her brothers, with my father's family and also between me and my children.

In fact I didn't even know that my father had brothers and sisters until I was in my mid-20s when my father was in the hospital. My uncle said that his brother wanted to come to see him. I asked, "What brother?" At that time, I learned of a brother who lived in Texas. Still, I didn't learn about other siblings until my father's sister crossed over. I never knew he had a sister, and she lived in the next town from me.

At one point, my mother had my sister not speaking to me...and to this day, I have a brother who I have not seen or heard from in 30 years. He lives in same state where I live.

I grew up in the late 50s and early 60s when no one talked about things that went on in one's family. I was told, "What is said in this house stays in this house." I have to laugh about it now, because there was hardly anything said.

In 1988 I met a cousin, on my father's side, at an uncle's funeral. I learned that she lived two blocks behind me. I called her, asking why I didn't know that my father had brothers and sisters. She told me that my mother caused a lot of trouble with his side of the family. One incident involved a deed that apparently she held onto, resulting in my grandmother not being able to be buried alongside my grandfather. They are buried in separate cemeteries.

## Current Life Reasons

In another session, Jeff tried to take me back into memories of being in the womb. I couldn't get there; I could only go back to around age three. He directed me to find my mother, and I went into the kitchen. I saw her, standing at the stove stirring a large pot, perhaps making soup. I could tell she was angry and I heard her mumbling some words about her mother. I could see she was becoming more and more upset.

Jeff was in my house, on another occasion, discussing a business arrangement. I was in the kitchen and he was sitting in the sunroom. Unexpectedly, he spoke up, "Your mother (spirit) is here." I cringed and commented, "Oh, really." I still stayed in the kitchen, out of his view, listening to what he was saying.

Jeff tuned in to her psychically. He told me that before I was born, my mother was having an affair with a police officer. One weekend when my father came home, on leave, my father "bedded her down," (mother's words) and she became pregnant with me. Therefore, she had to break off the affair. It hit me like a lead balloon. I thought, *This is it!* This was why she always hated me...because she had to break off the affair!

It also brought back the memory of her telling me that we had an uncle who was a police officer. I remembered this man, in a uniform, coming to our house—I thought he was my uncle. Back in those days, as a show of respect, we never called an adult by their first name. It was always "aunt" or "uncle."

Forgiveness does not come easy; I'm still in the process of forgiving her. With all the pain, she was still my mother, and I do love her. There are still things, to this day, which come up, and I get angry all over again. I am very sensitive to what people say, because it brings me right back to my mother's words.

I recognize now that it is my mother who gave me the strength to make me who I am today. She had to be strong to lose both parents at such a young age and become responsible for the rest of her family. She raised three children, primarily on her own. Alcoholism and mental problems reflected the baggage that she carried.

When we hang on to the hurts of the past, the baggage gets heavier and heavier. Life is so short; with all that goes on around us, if we can forgive, let go and enjoy it, we will be happier.

◊◊◊

Gail's honesty is refreshing. Too often people exclaim, "Oh, all you have to do is forgive." When there is deep pain, it is simply not as easy as that. First one has to go through the emotional hurt, anger, or grief—acknowledge and release it. Without that, forgiveness becomes a mental exercise and has no value. Only after healing the emotional and mental energies, can one move to higher levels of spiritual understanding and forgiveness.

How does one know if s/he has truly forgiven the person? They will recognize that forgiveness has taken place when there is no more energy (anger, hurt, grief) that is triggered...when there is a true detachment from the person and memories of the past. That does not mean the person no longer remembers; it means that they are no longer stuck in the emotional quagmire of the memories.

# Making Sense of It All

In my work as a psychic medium, I have come across a great many skeptics. I have found myself defending, to countless people, the job I do. Some of them have valid arguments for their position.

Sadly, there are many skeptics who are only skeptical because they do not understand the spiritual world. There is a lot of nonsense attached to psychic work and even from a medium's point of view, it is easy to see how people can find the whole thing a bit far-fetched.

The amount of television shows, films and fictional books about the paranormal has led to views of spirits that are grossly exaggerated, some to the point of foolishness. Over the years I have encountered several hair-raising situations, but I have never been slimed with green stuff called ectoplasm or summoned by the devil. It is only common sense to recognize the dramatic works of fiction must have hyper-realistic situations in order to satisfy their audiences. They are *not*, and I assume are not intended to be, accurate or honest representations of the subject matter.

On many occasions I have had people call me to cancel their appointment because they watched something on TV, such as *Scariest and Haunted Castles*. I've had a few fearful that if they came for their appointment, they might take home an entity like a poltergeist (a disruptive ghost or spirit that makes its presence known by noise, knocking, or moving objects). Most likely, if the appointment had been kept, he or she would have heard from their Uncle Joe or Aunt Claudia.

Terminology is a source of confusion, too. I commonly use the word, "energy". When mediums talk about energy, they are referring to the particular spirit that is coming in. We can all tell when someone is having a bad day or is in a bad mood; we can just feel it. That is also what I mean by energy. I use the word energy instead of saying vibes.

If someone walks into a house and feels unease, for no apparent reason, most likely they are picking up on energy of the house, or feeling emotions that were expressed or released many years ago in the house. This is what I call residual energy; it remains long after the property has been vacated, like having residue in a tub after taking a bath.

Another misunderstanding is that *not all spirits are ghosts.* Again, it's a matter of terminology – I view ghosts as spirits.

When I contact a loved one for someone during a reading, I sometimes see them in the clothing they wore; sometimes it is what they liked most. I never see feet, but there are times when they show me shoes. When I have asked about shoes they show me and I've been told it was their favorite pair. I transfer their messages to their loved ones here on earth. They are on another plane, which is another layer of existence.

I've done readings for many people who referred to themselves as skeptic. When they initially tell me that they are skeptical, I thank them for being honest. By the end of their reading, they have told me that they will come back...and do.

On the other hand, I've had a few people who try to test me. They are the ones who give yes or no responses with no additional feedback. It pulls on my energy; I'm giving information (energy) out and getting nothing back. When this happens, I stop the reading. My energy is important to me and I have learned how to value it.

## Psychic Accuracy

Sometimes, especially when my energies are low, I have been known to *get my wires crossed...*or as I call it, "Aunt Clara mode." On the TV show, "Bewitched," Aunt Clara was the very confused relative of Samantha who was always getting her wires crossed and getting into trouble.

◊◊◊

Gail's humorous description reminds us that psychics are human...and none are 100% accurate 100% of the time. There is an "energy dance" that is always taking place and as Gail indicates she has to pay attention to her energy. That advice is true for everyone. Valuing and noticing one's physical health (eating healthy food, exercising, and getting rest and sleep) – emotional health, and mental health is a necessity to one's clarity in intuitive perception. When we are "in alignment" our *channel* to the spirit world is clearer.

As our book comes to conclusion, Gail shares where she is in her life now...and it will surprise many readers who didn't fully grasp the power of her words, "it is my belief that hell is here on earth" It has been true for her.

As I've explained, our soul memories, genes from our parents, and experiences since birth are in our physical DNA. When one's life has been traumatic and lacking in love, we need to understand that healing can sometimes take "a lifetime." Nevertheless, that is our task — to heal from the past – and to bring our spirits into our bodies in order to live *Heaven On Earth.*

## My Life Today

After all my trials and tribulations, I am still surviving. Who would ever guess that I have faced thousands of people doing *Angels Among Us: A Spiritual Enlightenment with Gail Lionetti.* In these events, I communicate with loved ones who have crossed over, giving peace and closure to those in my audience.

In surviving all that I've experienced in my life, I have never lost faith. If we have no faith...we have nothing.

That doesn't mean that my life is perfect. Some days I am overwhelmed by others' grief and turmoil as they reach out to me. During those times, I can go into a deep depression.

In my work, picking up on other people's sadness and grief can pull me down. Often people have said, "I wish I had your gift." In reading this book, I trust that you understand that it is not as easy as you may have thought.

This depression occurred during the concluding writing of this book. Between the external demands upon me and my internal thoughts, I actually thought of taking my own life. This will shock the many people who know me and think that I'm so strong.

In the midst of this—in fact, on the day that I considered taking my life—I picked up the local newspaper [see article in Appendix] from my front door and read the headlines on the front page:

*On a Wing and a Prayer.*

In addition to the headline being the title of this book, the article was about the eagle no longer being extinct. The picture of the beautiful eagle, I felt, was a sign from my guides to *straighten up, fast*. My thoughts were that the eagle represents union, strength and pride in who we are. It was endangered but was able to regain its strength with love, care and protection from us. Similar to the eagle, it is our friends and loved ones who will protect, love and comfort us until we can regain strength and be ready to "soar" by ourselves.

I knew they were watching over me. It was no coincidence; I was in awe. My tears stopped immediately!

# Appendix

# ON A WING AND A PRAYER

The bald eagle – the national bird since 1782 – is rebounding after DDT nearly rendered it extinct

A bald eagle flies across trees at the Manasquan Reservoir. The birds remain on the federal threatened species list.
(PRESS FILE PHOTOS)

By KATHY MATHESON
STAFF WRITER

Six years ago this week, environmentalists seemingly had cause to rejoice: President Clinton proposed taking the bald eagle off the federal threatened and endangered species list.

The symbol of American strength and pride, whose numbers had been decimated by use of the pesticide DDT after World War II, had rebounded through nationwide conservation efforts and no longer was considered threatened.

Yet today, the eagle remains on the threatened list and is likely to stay on it for at least another year, said Cindy Hoffman, spokeswoman for the U.S. Fish & Wildlife Service.

Agency officials have not yet finished a set of proposed guidelines for managing the species once it is no longer protected, Hoffman said.

Being on the list provides certain safeguards for the eagle; if removed, the bird will continue to need some protection, she explained.

"We still stand behind our original proposal of 1999 that the species is ready to be taken off of the

See **Eagles**, Page **A9**

**APP.COM** Visit our Web site and click on the Web Extras button for a link to the National Wildlife Federation – American Bald Eagle.

183

# Practice ends as dog finds real body

## Alpine exercise takes grim turn

By **ELISE YOUNG**
Staff Writer

ALPINE — For three dogs trained to find bodies, an outing Monday in Palisades Interstate Park began as an ordinary refresher.

For several hours, their handlers — all officers with the Bergen County Sheriff's Office — drilled the German shepherds in the commands that make them indispensable at crime scenes.

Then, about 2:40 p.m., one dog came across the real thing.

Returning from a treacherous ravine near State Line Lookout, the dog, Baxter displayed "an extreme change in behavior," Undersheriff Jay Alpert said.

So Baxter's handler, Sgt. Michael Bradley, followed the dog hundreds of rocky feet down the cliff, where a clothed skeleton lay.

"The sergeant was down there, but didn't get all that terribly close," Alpert said.

With a nor'easter heading to North Jersey and the remains in such a remote location, authorities decided to delay the investigation until today. The remains were under police guard throughout the night.

On a cursory inspection, investigators could not determine the sex of the remains or ascertain how long they have been in the ravine, a remote section of cliff near the Hudson River, off Exit 2 of the Palisades Interstate Parkway.

Baxter's handler, who was at the scene late Monday, could not be reached for comment. For the dog, though the discovery was nothing out of the ordinary.

In August, he found a lost teenager, alive but suffering from snakebites, in a wooded section of Sussex County. In April, he found the body of a missing Garfield man not far from where he had parked on watershed property in Jefferson.

In 1995, the dog was part of a team scouring a wooded area of Nanuet, N.Y., to seek more possible victims of convicted murderer Reginald McFadden, who authorities believe was a serial killer. The dogs found nothing.

On Monday, neither Alpert nor Bergen County Prosecutor William H. Schmidt could speculate whether the remains might be those of one of McFadden's victims.

"It's absolutely 100 percent impossible to say at this time," Alpert said.

184

# Letter from Mary as described in A Born Again Comedian

Dear Gail,

We are so saddened to hear the defeat in your heart. We know it must be difficult to go through it all again. It is very important you not let your heart be so troubled. We are all faced with a series of Great Opportunities Brilliantly disguised as impossible situations. You are one of "God's Best" doing some of "His Best" deeds for all that you can! Truly you are needed here to do more of the same. I believe you've only just scratched the surface of what God has for you. Don't Believe the lies of the mind. It is only a brilliantly disguised deception of what we as Christians call the enemy. God's Word instructs us to believe in the Great Physician "The Holy Spirit"!

Casting all your care upon Him;
for He careth for you.   - 1 peter 5:7

And the peace of God, which passed all understanding,
shall keep your hearts and minds through Christ Jesus. -phil. 4:7

My peace I give unto to you. Let not your heart be troubled, neither
let it be afraid.    -jn. 14:27

You are Gail, and you will be now an even greater Testimony . Be confident in this!

And we know all things work together for good to them that Love God,
to them who are the called according to His Purpose. -rom 8:28

I pray that out of His glorious riches He may strengthen you with power through His Spirit in your inner being.   eph. 3:16

Be ready Gail...He is taking you to and even Higher level.

Launch out into the deep!   -luke 5:4

In His Strength,

# Tips for Getting a Good Reading

There is an art to getting a good psychic reading. Whether you're reading for yourself or someone else, you can help make the reading more relevant and valuable by being a little prepared and having a *driving question* or purpose for the reading. The tools you or the reader choose will, to some extent, define or limit the answers you can expect– the Runes, Tarot and I-Ching will probably all give the same general answer to the same question. However, the amount of intimacy, direction and depth you can obtain from any of these sources will depend not only on the reader's ability with that particular medium, but also the medium itself.

For example, unless you are a student of the I-Ching and able to read into the depths of each of the hexagrams and the lines that comprise them, you will find the medium limited– information concise and clear, but not voluminous. Reading the Tarot for the same question, especially a complex issue, can provide a great deal of data in comparison to the I-Ching. Even the novice Tarot reader can quickly begin to see times, people and events influencing the situation from a small layout.

So, the first lesson in getting a good reading is to get familiar with the different tools and understand how they are used, even if you never intend to read Tarot for someone else. If you find Tarot readings from others have produced good guidance for you, it's worth your taking some time to learn a little about it so you can relate better to what your reader is telling you. Avoid doing a reading when you're down– unless that's what you want the reading to be focused on.

While a reading in the midst of a crisis can be useful in helping you figure out how to deal with it, it's definitely not the best time for a life reading, since anything that shows up at the moment will be influenced by the crisis. It's best to wait until the dust has settled before you take a long-range view of your life. Birthdays and the beginning of a new year, whether it's January 1st, a new school year, or business year are all good times to choose a reading. Many of my clients come once a year around their birthday for a look at the upcoming year. Your decision is your own when to have a reading.

I'm often asked for lucky numbers to play the lottery, horse races and sports. However, if I were able to make such predictions accurately every day, I can assure you, I wouldn't be working so hard!

Psychics can provide good insight and information, guidance, and second opinions; but, they can not run your life. Even the most serious professionals certainly don't want to run your life. Use a reading as an additional source of information. Then, take your power and use your own instincts and intuition to know how best and when to apply what you learned from the reading.

### Some Do's and Don'ts for getting a good reading, from yourself or someone else.

**Do** create a "Sacred space", a quiet place for your reading. Burn some candles to keep the energy moving. Carry some crystals that you can set on the table during the reading; make sure the air is fresh and there are no distractions. Try to get away from your normal working environment into a place that's neutral.. Leave the children with a sitter if you can; their energy is strong and erratic and can easily distract a reader.

**Do** prepare yourself and have a purpose for the reading. Every psychic cringes when s/he asks a client what he or she wants to know about and the answer is 'the future.' The future is a very broad subject. Such an answer makes it hard for your reader to define the scope of the reading and focus on what's important to you now. So, for your next reading prepare a list of questions; then, prepare yourself before you begin. Take a few deep breaths, ground yourself, and try to generate some loving peaceful energy around you. Clear your mind of the cares and worries of the day. Then, clear your heart and will of your projections and expectations. When you want or wish for something so badly, a psychic can pick those desires as being in your future when in reality it's only you wishing so hard.

**Don't** expect a serious reading unless you're taking it seriously. If you've been taking alcohol or drugs, it can be very difficult for even the best readers to wade though the fog to find the clear answers you're wanting. If you've just eaten a big meal, had a fight with your partner, or you're not feeling well, these also can impact the quality and the tone of the reading. So, even if you're doing the reading "just for fun," take it a little seriously. Calm and clear yourself, even for a few minutes, before sitting down for the reading.

**Don't** expect the psychic to have eyes in the back of his or her head. The "Stump the Psychic" game that so many skeptics encourage as a first step in getting a good reading is a waste of your valuable time and money, and will often put even the best psychics off. Then, they are unable to 'perform' at all for you. I definitely encourage folks to be skeptical, especially when someone is offering spells or to remove curses, but it's truly a waste of time to hide your wedding rings, change your name or withhold information about your circumstances. If you are clear and direct with the reader about what's going on in your life and what you need to know right now, you'll have a much better chance of getting an accurate reading that provides you with some good guidance and direction.

### How do you tell if you've had a good reading?

Most psychics can tell within seconds of starting a reading, but there are three simple ways you can know when a reading is right.

1.  The reading feels complete. Completion means you have insight on what's going on around you, as well as information about what you can do about it. You have had clear answers to all of your questions. Most readers have a time limitation that you have paid for.

2.  You resonate with the reading. This means that the reader has accurately described you and the circumstances of your life and the events s/he predicts are possible in your life, given where you are now. On the orther hand, I've predicted events such as marriages, births, changes of staff, winnings and losses that our clients didn't believe possible, but occurred anyway. Readers can be very good at seeing those unexpected, unplanned, seemingly impossible

events that delight, surprise and sometimes take us back. But even then, I would distrust someone telling me I was about to win a million dollars if the rest of my reading didn't generally fit my life. However, if the rest of the reading resonates, I'd be out buying the ticket in a flash.

3.  You feel good when the reading has been completed, even if the reader has told you something you didn't want to hear. 'He's not coming back dear' is one of our most difficult and least well-received messages. If your reader is delivering bad news, she should also be delivering you some information about how to cope, what the purpose of this event is, how you can avoid or minimize it, and what the positive effects of this event will be in the long run. Otherwise, take the information with a grain of salt; refuse to be led by it and don't go back to that reader again. Every good psychic is also a healer and a reading is intended to be a healing experience. So, if you don't come away feeling good, then it probably wasn't a good reading.

Remember, a good reading is complete, feels right, and makes you feel good.

## To Contact Gail or Janet:

## Gail Lionetti

Web site: www.GailLionetti.com

## Janet Cunningham

Web sites: www.JanetCunningham.com
www.HeritageAuthors.com

Printed in the United States
42012LVS00006B/1-147

9 781420 892529